JAPAN

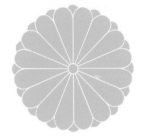

KURIL ISLANDS
(under dispute with the U.S.S.R.)

HOKKAIDO

• Sapporo

JAPANESE
ALPS

H

U

S

Mount Fuji

Tokyo •

JAPAN

By the Editors of Time-Life Books

TIME-LIFE BOOKS ○ ALEXANDRIA, VIRGINIA

Other Publications:

UNDERSTANDING COMPUTERS
YOUR HOME
THE ENCHANTED WORLD
THE KODAK LIBRARY OF CREATIVE
  PHOTOGRAPHY
GREAT MEALS IN MINUTES
THE CIVIL WAR
PLANET EARTH
COLLECTOR'S LIBRARY OF THE CIVIL WAR
THE EPIC OF FLIGHT
THE GOOD COOK
THE SEAFARERS
WORLD WAR II
HOME REPAIR AND IMPROVEMENT
THE OLD WEST
LIFE SCIENCE LIBRARY (revised)

This volume is one in a series of books
describing countries of the world —
their natural resources, peoples,
histories, economies and governments.

For information on and a full
description of any of the Time-Life
Books series listed above, please write:
Reader Information
Time-Life Books
541 North Fairbanks Court
Chicago, Illinois 60611

COVER: Outside the village of
Yoshida, on the west side of Honshu
Island, two women wearing
traditional headgear pause to exchange
comments while weeding rice
paddies irrigated with water channeled
from a mountain stream.

PAGES 1 AND 2: The emblem shown on
page 1 — a conventionalized form of
chrysanthemum flower, with 16
petals — is the chief crest of the
Japanese imperial family. The national
flag is shown on page 2.

ENDPAPERS: A topographic map
showing the mountainous nature of
the Japanese archipelago appears on
the front endpaper; the country is
made up of more than 3,000 islands.
The back endpaper shows the
regions and prefectures of Japan.

Time-Life Books Inc.
is a wholly owned subsidiary of

TIME INCORPORATED

FOUNDER: Henry R. Luce 1898-1967

Editor-in-Chief: Henry Anatole Grunwald
President: J. Richard Munro
Chairman of the Board: Ralph P. Davidson
Corporate Editor: Jason McManus
Group Vice President, Books: Reginald K. Brack Jr.
Vice President, Books: George Artandi

TIME-LIFE BOOKS INC.

EDITOR: George Constable
Executive Editor: George Daniels
Editorial General Manager: Neal Goff
Director of Design: Louis Klein
Editorial Board: Dale M. Brown, Roberta Conlan, Ellen
Phillips, Gerry Schremp, Donia Ann Steele, Rosalind
Stubenberg, Kit van Tulleken, Henry Woodhead
Director of Research: Phyllis K. Wise
Director of Photography: John Conrad Weiser

PRESIDENT: William J. Henry
Senior Vice President: Christopher T. Linen
Vice Presidents: Stephen L. Bair, Robert A. Ellis, John M.
Fahey Jr., Juanita T. James, James L. Mercer, Wilhelm
R. Saake, Paul R. Stewart, Christian Strasser

LIBRARY OF NATIONS

SERIES DIRECTOR: Dale M. Brown
Designer: Ray Ripper
Chief Researcher: Barbara Levitt
Editorial Staff for *Japan*
Associate Editors: David S. Thomson (text);
Sally Collins (pictures)
Text Editor: Roberta Conlan
Researchers: Denise Li (principal), Scarlet Cheng
Assistant Designer: Robert K. Herndon
Copy Coordinators: Margery duMond,
Robert M. S. Somerville
Picture Coordinator: Erin Monroney
Editorial Assistant: Myrna E. Traylor

Special Contributors: The chapter texts were written by:
Oliver Allen, Ezra Bowen, Walter Karp, Mayo Mohs,
Rafael Steinberg and Bryce Walker.
Other Contributors: Ann D. Corson, Martha George,
Rosemary George, Milton Orshefsky and Kazuhiro
Akimoto (translations).

Editorial Operations
Design: Ellen Robling (assistant director)
Copy Chief: Diane Ullius
Editorial Operations: Caroline A. Boubin (manager)
Production: Celia Beattie
Quality Control: James J. Cox (director), Sally Collins
Library: Louise D. Forstall

Correspondents: Elisabeth Kraemer-Singh (Bonn);
Margot Hapgood, Dorothy Bacon (London); Miriam
Hsia (New York); Maria Vincenza Aloisi, Josephine du
Brusle (Paris); Ann Natanson (Rome). Valuable
assistance was also provided by Dick Berry (Tokyo) and
Christina Lieberman (New York).

Assistant Editor for the U.S. Edition: Karin Kinney

OVERALL CONSULTANT

Susan J. Pharr, who has lived, studied and
worked in Japan, is an Associate Professor
of Political Science at the University of
Wisconsin. She has been a visiting fellow at
the University of Tokyo and a visiting
professor at Harvard University. Among
her numerous publications dealing with
Japan is a book, *Political Women in Japan.*

CONSULTANTS

Edwin O. Reischauer, one of the world's
leading experts on Japan, reviewed this
book. Dr. Reischauer served as United
States Ambassador to Japan between 1962
and 1966. He has written and lectured
widely on the country; among his books are
Japan Past and Present and *The Japanese.*

Dr. Merry I. White, the director of the
Project on Human Potential at Harvard
University, obtained her doctorate
from Harvard in 1980. She has visited
Japan often and has written about it in
various scholarly papers. Dr. White
reviewed Chapter 6.

First printing.

Printed in U.S.A.
Published simultaneously in Canada.
School and library distribution by Silver Burdett
Company, Morristown, New Jersey.

TIME-LIFE is a trademark of Time Incorporated U.S.A.

Library of Congress Cataloguing in Publication Data
Main entry under title:
Japan.
  (Library of Nations)
  Bibliography: p. 156
  Includes index.
  1. Japan. I. Time-Life Books. II. Series: Library of
Nations (Alexandria, Va.)
DS806.T222 1985   952   85-16478
ISBN 0-8094-5334-7
ISBN 0-8094-5121-2 (lib. bdg.)

In Japanese usage, surnames
precede given names. This practice has
been retained for well-known
historical figures in this book. However,
the Western style of name order
(surname last) has been used for
modern figures, as is customary in
most Western publications.

CONTENTS

Swimmers at the Korakuen amusement park in downtown Tokyo take an enforced break, one of three a day during which authorities reunite lost

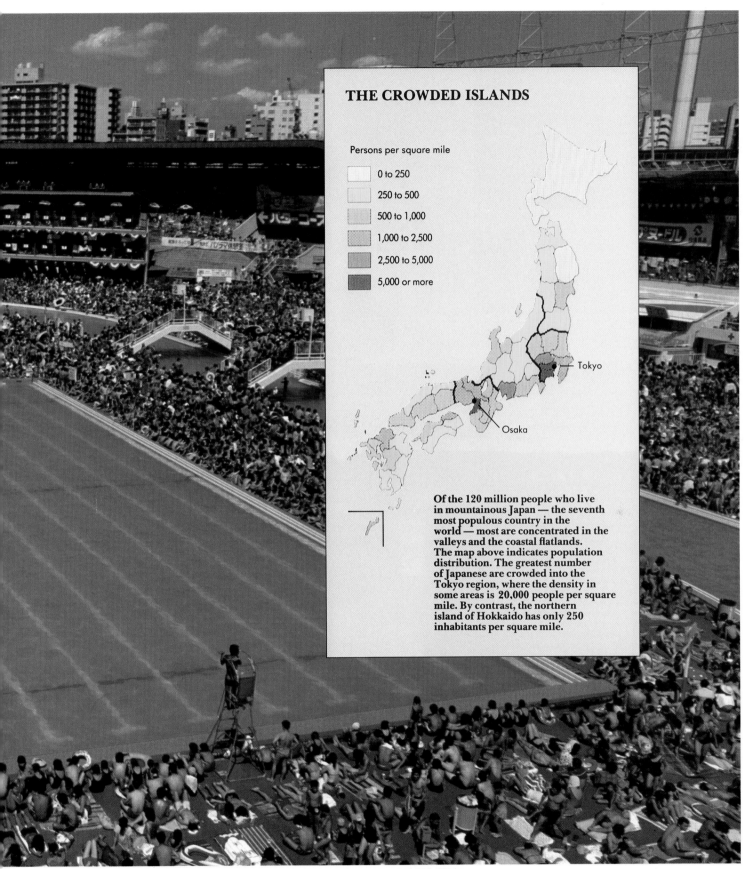

THE CROWDED ISLANDS

Persons per square mile

- 0 to 250
- 250 to 500
- 500 to 1,000
- 1,000 to 2,500
- 2,500 to 5,000
- 5,000 or more

Tokyo

Osaka

Of the 120 million people who live in mountainous Japan — the seventh most populous country in the world — most are concentrated in the valleys and the coastal flatlands. The map above indicates population distribution. The greatest number of Japanese are crowded into the Tokyo region, where the density in some areas is 20,000 people per square mile. By contrast, the northern island of Hokkaido has only 250 inhabitants per square mile.

children with their parents and treat injuries. The pool and moat can hold 30,000.

BIG YIELDS FROM SMALL FARMS

Though the average Japanese farm consists of only two and a half acres, it is a highly productive unit, as this chart attests. At the outset of the 20th Century, Japan produced only 80 per cent of the foodstuffs it consumed, and a growing population seemed certain to increase the dependency on imports.

Today, Japan is self-sufficient in rice, and nearly so in vegetables and fruits, but it imports large quantities of grain to feed animals raised for meat.

Farmers, with generous support from the government, now make heavy use of chemical fertilizers and scientific farming methods to increase productivity. In addition, those who live where the climate is mild plant two crops, a few even three crops, a year.

Domestic production

Domestic consumption

Million metric tons

25

20

15

10

5

0

RICE WHEAT LEGUMES VEGETABLES AND FRUITS MEAT

A farmer in a straw hat checks on the ripeness of his rice, Japan's biggest food crop. Almost 40 per cent of the country's arable land is given over to rice

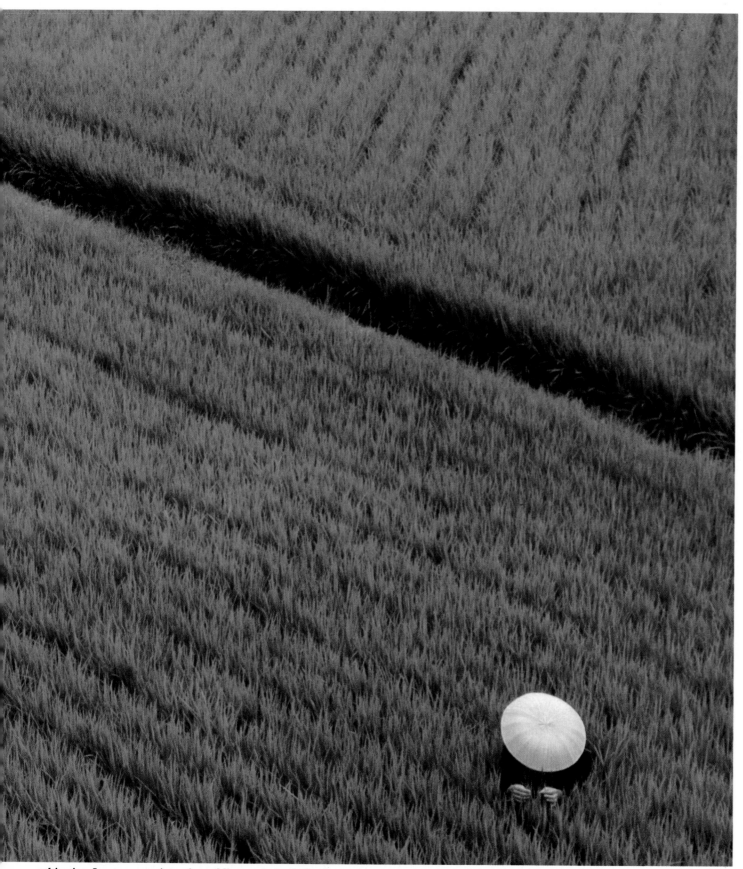

cultivation. In warmer regions, the paddies are drained after harvesting so that vegetables may be grown in them.

Surrounded by thousands of transistors, batteries, plugs and connectors, the owner of an electronics supply shop in Tokyo's Akihabara district takes a

PLUGGING INTO THE COMPUTER MARKET

Japan's rise to preeminence in the electronics field has been nothing short of meteoric. Sony was the first Japanese company to produce transistors, an invention borrowed from the Americans. That was in 1954; since then the Japanese electronics industry has grown at an extraordinary rate. There are 580 competing electronics companies in Japan today; in just one specialty area alone, memory chips for computers, Japan produces more than half of the world's supply.

Part of this success has to do with the willingness of the government, through the Ministry of International Trade and Industry (MITI), to encourage new technology by putting seed money into various companies. But the companies themselves, minding the dictum that "in business, you have to look ahead," have poured money of their own into development. The payoff promises to be handsome: By 1990, for example, the Japanese expect to have a 30 per cent share of the world computer market — a tripling of their share in the space of a decade.

telephone order. His shop caters to small manufacturers and to a few private individuals who build their own electronic equipment, including computers.

Schoolboys in rainwear squat while waiting for a school bus. No effort will be made during the first nine years of their education to separate out the

THE WORLD'S MOST EDUCATED PEOPLE

Japan's rigorous system of education has been called the best in the world. Everyone must attend school for 5½ days a week, 240 days a year for at least nine years. And though high school is voluntary, more than 90 per cent of Japanese youngsters now complete the three-year course. One measure of the efficacy of the Japanese system is the performance of 10- and 14-year-olds on standardized tests given to the children of 19 industrialized nations; the Japanese scored highest in most subjects.

No education

Completed compulsory education

Completed twelfth grade

Post high school education

100%

100%

100%

100%

1980

1970

1960

1950

gifted for special classes. Struggling students receive the help of their classmates.

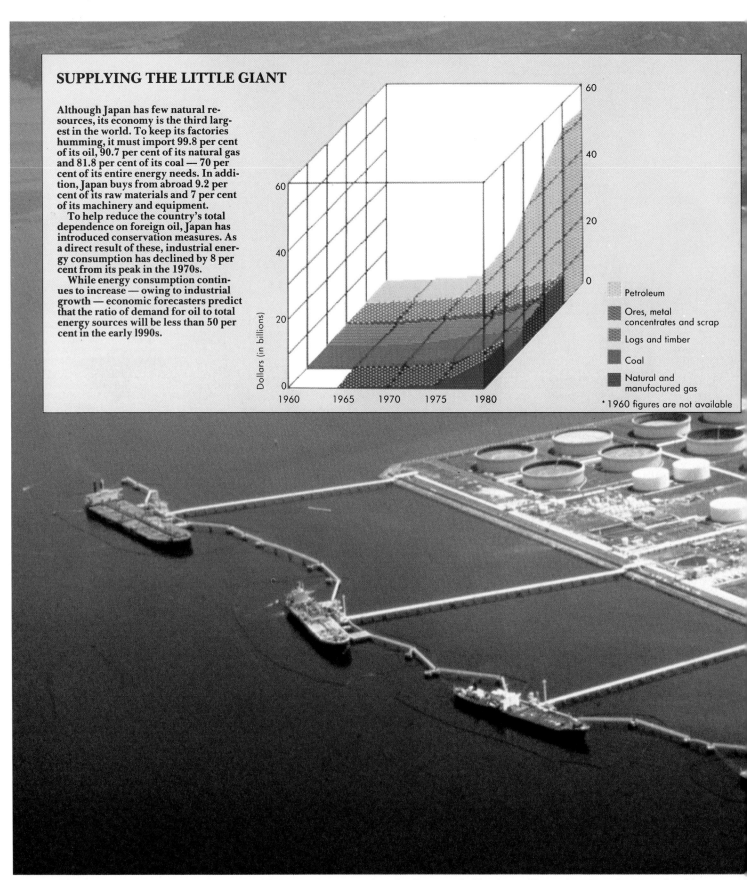

SUPPLYING THE LITTLE GIANT

Although Japan has few natural resources, its economy is the third largest in the world. To keep its factories humming, it must import 99.8 per cent of its oil, 90.7 per cent of its natural gas and 81.8 per cent of its coal — 70 per cent of its entire energy needs. In addition, Japan buys from abroad 9.2 per cent of its raw materials and 7 per cent of its machinery and equipment.

To help reduce the country's total dependence on foreign oil, Japan has introduced conservation measures. As a direct result of these, industrial energy consumption has declined by 8 per cent from its peak in the 1970s.

While energy consumption continues to increase — owing to industrial growth — economic forecasters predict that the ratio of demand for oil to total energy sources will be less than 50 per cent in the early 1990s.

Dollars (in billions)

1960   1965   1970   1975   1980

Petroleum

Ores, metal concentrates and scrap

Logs and timber

Coal

Natural and manufactured gas

* 1960 figures are not available

Tankers offload their precious cargo at Kiire, the world's largest aboveground crude-oil storage facility, located in southern Kyushu. More than 50 per

14

cent of every barrel of imported oil is used for industrial purposes.

Names of world-famous Japanese products light up the Tokyo night sky, along with those of two major department stores — Keio and Odakyu. To the left,

opposite the sign with the letters TDK, is the entrance to one of the city's entertainment districts.

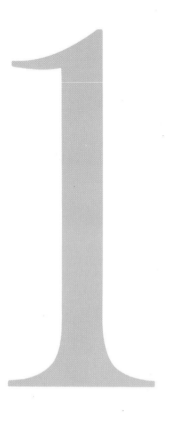

To have a garden like this one is a utopian
dream of every Japanese. But with living
space at a premium in a crowded nation of
120 million people, most gardens are, as one
Japanese put it, "the size of a cat's forehead."

OUT OF ASHES,
A NEW NATION

In the winter of 1974 a young Japanese adventurer named Norio Suzuki set off for the island of Lubang in the northwest Philippines, fascinated by tales of an elusive, death-dealing hermit who stalked the jungle trails in a World War II Japanese Army uniform. During a long series of sniper attacks, 30 Filipinos had been killed and 100 wounded. The uniform indicated that the sharpshooter was a last holdout of the once-victorious Japanese forces that had conquered the Philippines in 1942.

Arriving on Lubang, Suzuki camped in the jungle and eventually managed to contact this lethal recluse. He turned out indeed to be a Japanese soldier, Lieutenant Hiroo Onoda of Army Intelligence. He had known the War was over, he told Suzuki, but he nevertheless had felt it his duty to honor his Army orders never to give himself up. "Only in case my commanding officer rescinds my order in person will I surrender," he declared.

One of Onoda's military superiors, former Major Yoshimi Taniguchi, was located and willingly journeyed to Lubang. There Taniguchi read a 28-year-old directive that relieved Onoda, formally and honorably, of his duty. With a bow to the major, Lieutenant Onoda put down his gun and agreed to turn over his rusted officer's sword to Philippine President Ferdinand Marcos. At a brief ceremony in Manila, Marcos handed the sword back to Onoda, proclaimed him "a great soldier" and issued a pardon for all the crimes the lieutenant had committed. Onoda was then escorted to a plane that took him back at last to his beloved Japan, where more than 4,000 people crowded the arrival gates of Tokyo's Narita Airport to cheer the ultimate warrior.

Proudly erect in a new blue suit, Onoda emerged from the aircraft into modern Japan. He was the incarnation of a past made all the more remote by the enormous changes that had overtaken his homeland during his three decades in the Philippines.

What greeted the eyes of the man from the past was a vibrant new Japan, abounding with industry and material wealth. Since Onoda had gone to war, Tokyo had been transformed from a largely wooden city of five million to an awesome steel-and-concrete metropolis of more than 15 million. Streets that in the 1940s had borne bicycles and rattling trucks by 1974 rumbled beneath the weight of several million Japanese-built motor vehicles — most of them private cars. Most women moved briskly through the streets in high heels and modish Western dresses or pants suits. Booming metal foundries and chemical complexes lined suburban superhighways in areas once covered by peaceful quiltworks of rice paddies. And upon a meticulously constructed, computer-controlled track, a gleaming blue-and-white bullet train whipped along at speeds of 125 miles per hour and more.

The rest of Japan moved apace. During Onoda's long, self-imposed exile, the old island kingdom had emerged as an economic superpower. By the mid-1970s its resurgent industries were outproducing those of France, West Germany and Great Britain. Not only automobiles, but also television sets, tape recorders and stereo equipment streamed off production lines — for export and also for home consumption, as the Japanese themselves had become adept and eternally eager consumers.

In short, the Japan Lieutenant Onoda had left in the mid-1940s had undergone a metamorphosis unprecedented for speed and thoroughness. Japan had hardly been a backward nation when it launched itself into World War II; it had already outstripped its Asian neighbors in industry and trade — and armaments. But it had been a country of frugal people, dominated by the figures of the hard-working farmer, fisherman and small merchant. The Japan Onoda came back to had all the glitter of one of the world's wealthiest nations. "In our history of 2,000 years," said a member of Japan's Diet (or parliament), "this is the first time that the Japanese have not had to worry about poverty. We are *nouveau riche*, a nation of farmers only a short time ago."

All these changes were too much for Onoda, who came from a traditional small-town family. Unsettled by the glitter and distressed by Japan's growing materialism, he became an exile again. Moving to an outlying district of a distinctly less bustling and less industrialized nation, Brazil, he settled down on a small cattle ranch. "Everyone back in Japan is concerned with money," he said; "I cannot live like that."

Most other members of Lieutenant Onoda's generation and their children have found being *nouveau riche* gratifying. By the mid-1980s, most of Japan's people enjoyed to the full the fact that they possessed amenities and advantages befitting a society as advanced as any on earth. The average annual income of a Japanese family had climbed to $20,000. The unemployment rate stood at a minuscule 2.7 per cent. More than 99 per cent of all households contained refrigerators and color television sets. Two out of three families owned a passenger car and at least one tape recorder; more than 8 of every 10 had electric sewing machines. And about 40 per cent of all Japanese homes were equipped with air conditioners or microwave ovens.

To view this new Japanese consumerism — and especially the insatiable appetite for electronic wares — at its gaudiest, the shopper needed only to visit Tokyo's Akihabara bazaar. This blaring complex of shops and discount caves engulfing 20 blocks in the north-central section of the city specializes in the products of Japan's hundreds of murderously competitive electronics companies. Here shouting pitchmen, rotating come-on lights and mammoth montages of pricing cards have created one of the most uninhibited commercial extravaganzas on earth. A single store in this bargain hunters' mecca recently carried no fewer than 100 different models of color television sets, more than 200 kinds of headphones and 75 sorts of record-player turntables.

Some Japanese have echoed Onoda in deploring such blatant materialist excess, feeling that Japan's ancient spiritual and moral values are in danger of being buried under an avalanche of machines and gadgets. But in a recent poll, an astounding 89 per cent of the people pronounced themselves basically contented with their lives.

Whether for good or ill, the economic strides made by Japan since World War II constitute nothing less than a miracle. Japan has risen literally from its own ashes. When the War ended in 1945 and Lieutenant Onoda's comrades came home, they found that virtually all the major cities had been burned out by 90,000 tons of bombs, mostly incendiaries, dropped from U.S. Air Force B-29s. Two cities had been almost completely obliterated by atom bombs. Industry had been hammered flat and 10 million people were unemployed. Farm output had fallen by almost one half and many of the defeated country's people faced the real threat of starvation. Across the nation's ruins raged a typhoon of inflation that would cause prices to rise 600-fold between 1945 and 1950.

The road back from such desperate circumstances was paved from the very first with good intentions on the part of victor and vanquished alike. Even more astonishing, the intentions were matched by deeds and by a growing sense of comradeship that, if occasionally frayed, has remained strong. The Japanese had expected the worst from the Allied Occupation forces, but they were pleasantly surprised when the Supreme Commander, U.S. General Douglas MacArthur, after imposing new rules, indicated in 1945 that Japan would govern itself. He initiated an agricultural reform bill that transferred ownership of a large portion of the country's producing acreage from the long-entrenched landlords to the farmers themselves. He also broke up the *zaibatsu*, the great industrial complexes. Even more radically, MacArthur's young staff bestowed upon Japan a new democratic constitution.

Among other key provisions, the

constitution set forth a bill of rights along American lines, gave women the right to vote and lowered the voting age, refashioned the Diet into a popularly elected Western-style parliament and turned Emperor Hirohito from a celestial ruler into a benign "symbol of the state," who at last was free to pursue his heart's passion of research in marine biology. Shortly thereafter, the United States made clear its intent to see Japan rebuilt into an Asian "bulwark of democracy" and the "workshop of the Far East." The United States then removed the last bars to economic growth by canceling all but token payments of war reparations.

From this point on, superb management and unceasing hard work (Akio Morita and Masaru Ibuka started the electronic giant Sony by grubbing radio equipment parts from the rubble of bombed buildings) began to generate the brilliant success that is present-day Japan. The Korean War was to provide a critical push. That conflict brought a bonanza of hundreds of millions of dollars in foreign exchange, to pay for Japanese-made trucks and other heavy equipment as well as housing and services for the United Nations troops who operated supply bases in Japan, and for units passing through on their way to the Korean fighting.

As a result, by 1955 Japanese industry had all but recovered from its defeat in 1945. The Japanese government proceeded to step in with an effective five-year plan for national growth that included tariff protection and subsidies for key industries. With the government's help and blessing, huge new steel, shipbuilding and manufacturing complexes were formed by a fresh generation of industrial leaders.

In a way these burgeoning industries

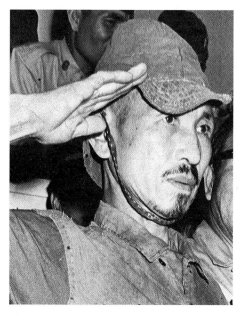

benefited from the destruction wreaked during World War II. New and highly efficient factories rose from the rubble of the old. Within 20 years the Japanese were forging steel in their up-to-date furnaces at a lower cost per ton than most world producers, and Japanese shipyards had become marvels of cost-efficient production. By the late 1970s Japan boasted a gross national product equal to France's and England's combined.

Shrewdly, the Japanese reinvested huge proportions of their gross national product — as much as 32 per cent a year between 1956 and 1960 — in order to modernize old industries and bankroll new ones. Helped by such massive financial boosts, the nation's car and truck production soared from 100,000 units in 1960 to two million in 1970. During the early 1970s Japan rivaled West Germany as the world's No. 2 automobile maker. Again, efficient plants and eager workers added up to remarkable productivity. By 1977, the average Japanese autoworker made 33 cars per year, versus 26 per year for an American; and the Toyotas and Datsuns sold at retail prices averaging $1,500 less per car. Almost one fourth

of the United States auto market had by 1980 gone over to Japanese-made cars.

At the same time, Japan's light industry grew to surpass the Swiss in the production of watches and the Germans in cameras, lenses and optical equipment. The Japanese also carved out a large share of the world market for such disparate items as bicycles, skiing gear and consumer electronic goods. In 1983 total output surpassed a trillion dollars per year, as Japan had become not only America's principal commercial rival, but also the biggest or second-biggest trading partner of every nation in Southeast Asia.

A main motive force behind this astonishing climb to commercial dominance has come from the Japanese workers themselves. Probably no other people on earth throw themselves into their jobs with comparable devotion and energy. Japanese companies foster their employees' morale and productivity with devices that range from pep rallies to "voluntary speedups."

At Matsushita, a giant of the electronics industry, the workers in the main plants for years assembled in groups each morning to sing the company song right through to its rousing end: "Sending our goods to the people of the world/Endlessly and continuously/Like water gushing from a fountain./Grow, industry, grow, grow, grow!" They still recite the company creed, which includes the lines, "Alone we are weak, together we are strong. We shall work together as a family in mutual trust and responsibility."

Toyota employs similar spurs. The company's weekly newsletter exhorts the workers to "challenge the highest peaks with our all-out efforts," and a mouth-filling corporate slogan continually reminds them that "With ingenu-

ity and good ideas, we can find a solution to increased orders even beyond our present full capacity." And they do; in 1980 Toyota reduced its main plant's transmission-assembly time to a whirlwind 45 seconds, and in the course of three years had lowered the time it took to pack certain parts for shipment from an hour to 12 minutes.

Meanwhile archrival Nissan, the maker of Datsun trucks and cars, organized worker volunteers into some 4,000 quality-control teams. One team offered to eliminate down time on machines by staying after hours for the service and cleanup that normally had been taken out of the final period of the day's run. Other teams have engaged in production experiments: "First we work one machine with the left hand, then another with the right," a quality-control volunteer explained. "Then we put one machine in front and another behind and work them simultaneously." During 1980 alone the volunteers chopped 13.6 billion yen, then worth $60 million, from Nissan's assembly costs, assisting the company toward profits the following year of 158.7 billion yen, or $700 million.

The devotion of Japanese workers to their company's success extends to the nation's labor unions. The unions stage periodic rallies at which a great deal of noisy rhetoric is aired, and they do succeed in bargaining for higher wages. But in most corporations the unions' main function is to keep things calm, lest the ever-rising heat of production generate a labor explosion. As a former union president phrased it, "The bluebird of happiness does not dwell in the swamps of spite where the storms of struggle rage."

Criticizing the company or the union can be costly. One worker with the temerity to question a union wage position found himself shunned by his friends, who had been warned that association with him could poison their own futures. The man himself now makes some $2,000 per year less than his quieter fellows.

Such disharmony is very rare, however; most Japanese manage to put on a good face for the factory, without compulsion or undue inner effort. The general attitude seems to be encapsuled in the words of a Nissan employee: "I'll keep quiet and try to get promoted."

Japan's extraordinary economic gains have been achieved at a price — and not just of devoted and relentless work. There have been social costs as well. Growing industrialization has meant that the cities have burgeoned and grown stupefyingly crowded. Japan is a larger country than many non-Japanese think, stretching more than 2,000 miles from its northernmost island to its most southerly one; but the total geographical area is only about as large as Finland, and it is inhabited by about 120 million people (versus Finland's 4.8 million). Further, only 29 per cent of Japan's land is usable for living space, agriculture and industry combined; the rest is too mountainous. Crowding is so chronic that, in the phrase of former U.S. Ambassador Edwin O. Reischauer, Japan's "standard of well-being" is far lower than the country's standard of living would indicate. "You work in a modern building," said one government employee. "You eat in a good restaurant. You ride in a fast train. You come home at night and you have to be careful not to step on your sleeping kid's belly."

The one natural resource Japan needs most, but cannot import, is land. Because of this lack of livable space, most Japanese houses are small — by Western standards, cramped. The typical exurban family of four outside Tokyo, Kobe, Osaka or Nagoya lives in a three-room bungalow slightly larger than a two-car garage, the interior as tightly packed with gear as the inside of a weekend sailor's cabin cruiser. The family members sleep on bedding that can be stuffed away to turn the bedroom into a daytime living room-dining room — which may open onto a tiny back garden of raked pebbles, a few meticulously arranged rocks, some moss and a dwarf tree or two.

Japanese living in such modest retreats must spend up to four hours a day commuting to and from work. And the commuter trains, especially those serving Tokyo, are without doubt the most abominably crowded in the world. Tokyo's subways, for that matter, are just as bad; during rush hours the last bodies must be jammed aboard by a special breed of white-gloved platform attendants. Both train and subway riders accept this crowding with equanimity, simply relaxing and swaying with the crowd. "Millions of commuters ride trains as crowded as 19th Century slave ships," a Japanese once observed, "but show no signs of mutiny. Even with someone's newspaper shoved in their face and someone's elbow jammed in their side, they remain indifferent."

Crowding in the urban centers is even more relentless; one survey revealed that on workdays some parts of downtown Tokyo are packed with 38,000 people per square mile. The average city-dwelling couple must somehow make do in a tiny two-room apartment totaling 400 square feet.

With crowding have come environmental problems, including dirty air and water. Japan's rivers and harbors

Parked bumper to bumper, cars and vans await loading at a Nagoya dock. Japan exports nearly four million automobiles annually to 170 countries. Overseas car sales account for 13 per cent of Japan's gross national product.

1

Built helter-skelter, houses like these typify the overcrowding in cities and towns. Housing is considered the foremost social problem in Japan, where 17.7 per cent of available shelter falls below minimum standards set by the government.

have been polluted, not only by commercial wastes but by the horrendous quantities of garbage generated by this nation of freshly fledged but enthusiastic consumers. In recent years the Japanese government has made a concerted attack on the pollution of the nation's waterways — and has made considerable progress in cleaning up the air as well. As for the garbage pileup, the Japanese make do with ingenuity. One urban unit in Aichi prefecture, a heavily populated area between Tokyo and Kyoto, has attacked the problem by spraying its fleet of garbage trucks with perfumed deodorants. The Aichi garbage vans now smell like peppermint and broadcast sprightly music as they cruise through the streets.

The Japanese, indeed, meet all their urban problems — the crowding, the pollution, the relentless bustle of the big cities — with a cheerfulness and an elaborate politeness that help reduce the inevitable tensions of modern urban life. They also survive these problems and pressures in part through a special form of self-abnegation.

The Japanese tend to view themselves as members of a group, all working toward group goals, rather than as unique individuals striving for personal advancement. Indeed, the whole Western concept of struggling for individual freedom or special recognition is anathema to the Japanese. The American hero is the cowboy, who stands alone against the sky, no man's servant. The Japanese revere their warriors of old, the samurai, who vowed lifelong allegiance to a noble master. The Western concept is summed up in an old saw, "The squeaky wheel gets the grease." The comparable Japanese saying is, "The nail that sticks up gets pounded down."

Japanese society's governing ethic is embodied in an all-but-untranslatable concept called *on*. It derives from Confucian social philosophy borrowed long ago from China, whose fundamental precepts are mutual obligation and a respect for the natural hierarchy within human relationships. The typical Japanese is most comfortable knowing exactly where he or she stands relative to people above, below and on either side. When Japanese businesspeople meet,

they invariably exchange business cards in a bilateral status signal that governs the tenor of all their subsequent dealings. The white-collar worker derives pride and identity from carrying a company briefcase or wearing a company badge. Japanese men and women, like all other human beings, do harbor private ambitions, resentments and impulses to rebel, but they keep such feelings deep inside, in deference to the overriding primacy of the group.

In a country so small and so densely packed, this sense of shared obligation and of social duty is both a national blessing and a life necessity. Otherwise, like the creatures in the overpacked maze of a psychological experiment, the Japanese might erupt in violence. Instead, they take meticulous care to avoid confrontation. When faced with an uncongenial suggestion, a Japanese will respond, "I fully understand your cordial proposition," or simply, "Let me think it over," rather than making objections or saying, "No." The closest he will come to a negative may be a scratching of the head, accompanied by the extended syllable *"Saaaah"* — indicating that it will be hard to agree.

The Japanese white-collar worker — today universally called a *sarariman,* or "salaryman," in one of the many words the Japanese have adopted from English since the War — often seeks relief from the tensions of the workplace, as do many of his counterparts in the West, by visiting a bar before going home. Tokyo has 10,000 modest watering holes that cater to after-work groups of salarymen intent on relaxation and comradeship.

In lieu of alcohol, the work-frazzled young Japanese man may throw himself into marathon rounds of *pachinko,* a vertical pinball game. Or he may head off for a bout of hitting bucket after bucket of golf balls at a mechanized, multistoried driving range, a pastime that can be as frantic as the work from which he is trying to unwind.

In private the Japanese forgo such frenetic pursuits, gaining satisfaction from common things and from humble, very personal pursuits such as gardening. This is a felicity derived from their ancient religion, Shinto, which holds that all natural things are holy. The sound of wind in a pine and the reflection of a flower petal in a pond's surface are real treasures to a Japanese.

The people also enjoy intellectual pursuits. Thanks to the nation's excellent, awesomely demanding and universally attended school system — with 90 per cent of all boys and 91 per cent of girls graduating from high school — virtually all citizens, from the northern tip of Hokkaido to the last little islands south of Kyushu, can read. And they do, assiduously.

Some 93 per cent of all Japanese take one of the nation's 125 daily newspapers. Tokyo's enormously influential *Asahi Shimbun* and the rival *Yomiuri Shimbun* each claim daily circulations of more than 12 million, making them the world's two largest newspapers. On top of this, Japan's publishers produce more than 2,300 periodicals, ranging

A uniformed attendant helps load people onto a Tokyo subway train. Rush hour is referred to as "Transportation Hell" by the passengers; in the crush, riders have been known to lose shoes.

from scholarly journals to the immensely popular adult comic books — both lily-white and blue — called *manga*. A serious magazine of opinion, *Bungei Shunju,* sells an astonishing million copies per month. The Japanese also devour books; more than 40,000 new titles are published each year.

These various ways of coping with pressure appear to work, keeping a lid of serenity on a vibrating nation. In two of the surest indices of the human condition, longevity and violent crime, Japan enjoys some of the best ratings among the industrialized nations. Serious crime in Japan is relatively rare: In Tokyo in one recent year only 505 robberies were reported, compared with 7,585 in London — and a whopping 100,550 in New York. Life expectancy in Japan has now become longer than in most other developed countries. The average Japanese male lives to be 74, the average woman, 80.

In an increasingly white-collar society, the *sarariman* has become the quintessential figure in modern Japan, comparable to the straw-hatted farmer of the past, bent over his rice plants in an ankle-deep paddy. These "salarymen" make up only about one fourth of the male work force, but they constitute the army of salesmen, clerks and junior managers that keeps industrial Japan going and advancing. In his neat business suit, the *sarariman* resembles the ancient farmer in just one thing: He works as hard or harder, and with the same singleminded devotion.

When a young Japanese man fresh out of college joins a company — a degree from a prestigious university being the absolutely essential requirement for white-collar employment in a leading firm — he automatically becomes a *moretsu shain,* a passionate com-

pany man. He gets up at dawn or before — depending on the length of his commute — pushes down a Western-style breakfast and gets to his office at 8:30 sharp. Punctuality is a passion. "The company is feeding and keeping me, after all," one such worker has said; "it's the least I can do in return."

First thing on Mondays, the young employee joins the entire staff for the weekly pep rally; then he races to his desk, which is stuffed into a cramped warren of identical workspaces, to battle the morning's paperwork, receive orders and transmit them down the line. He lunches quickly on a snack of noodles or perhaps raw fish at some small place around the corner, then returns to his desk to work through the afternoon — and often until late into the evening. Many salarymen feel they cannot go home until the boss does, and many bosses are all too hard-working.

The young employee may not get home until almost midnight. For his devotion he is paid overtime.

When a young *sarariman* has moved a few rungs up the ladder — to the rank of manager, say, of a branch plant — his day may be even more strenuous. One such branch manager, with a tent-making firm in Osaka, usually spends his mornings at his desk, then calls on customers until 5:30 p.m. He then rushes off to a chamber of commerce meeting in his local prefecture, where the topic may be the worrisome failure of certain conservative, business-oriented candidates to win office in recent national elections. "Politics, after all," says the manager, "is bound to have an impact on business." Then he picks up two clients for a long, luxurious dinner. "I don't like entertaining," he admits privately, but adds that if he did not do it, he would "go to pieces in

Indulging their passion for pachinko, a game of skill in which winners receive prizes, men play the machines in one of Japan's 10,000 pachinko parlors. Most parlors are near mass-transit terminals, allowing commuters to play a couple of games after work.

business. That, naturally, is something I have to avoid, no matter what."

At about midnight he arrives home, to be greeted by his wife bearing two small cups and a pot of green tea, which they quietly share. Finally he peeks in upon his sleeping children before dropping into bed himself. Tomorrow will be the same.

The energy — as well as the propensity — for such devoted work seems to come from deep in the national gene pool. One visitor to Japan offered the following impression: "Everywhere brisk industry, a steady hustle and bustle, swarming in all the streets from early morning to late at night. Everywhere people are busily working, are busily studying. Everyone tries to outdo everyone else in achievement, in knowledge and in dexterity." That was written more than 400 years ago, but it rings true today.

In return for all his work and dedication, the *sarariman* expects the company to take care of him. And generally it does. The company president, besides his purely executive and commercial role, functions as a combination father and feudal lord. The employee becomes a kind of samurai-offspring, with the relationship governed by *on*.

The big Japanese firms are paternalistic to a degree unheard of anywhere else. In 1974 Matsushita suffered a sudden sales drop in color televisions so severe that 10,000 jobs became redundant. But the founder of the company announced that his employees were "treasures" and sent down an irrevocable order, "Never discharge them!" Instead, the entire payroll was put on half-time to ride out the recession — during which the grateful employees created a "Sales Volunteer Force" that sold out the company's inventory and

helped put Matsushita back in full operation within six months.

For such job security, however, and the assurance that seniority will be rewarded with steady advancement, the worker gives up having much of a life of his own. "You have an employer and you are a unit, a cell operating under his orders and directives," explains one *sarariman*. "You can't do what you'd like to." One whisky distillery, in its unceasing drive to foster the humility that Japan regards as the corollary to productivity, offers an annual Greatest Confession Prize to the person who admits to the year's prime corporate blunder — perhaps losing an account through poor negotiations, or making a bad technical decision that shut down the production line.

Japanese white-collar workers tolerate all this because their work ethic includes a remarkable devotion to famil-

WESTERN SPORTS
OF MASS APPEAL

Skiers crowd the slopes of Mount Takenoko in the Naeba Mountains of central Japan. Since the facility is relatively close to Tokyo and Osaka, it has become one of the nation's premier ski resorts.

Sadaharu Oh holds the world record for home runs — 868 in all.

Golfers improve their strokes at a Tokyo practice center. Because membership

Though characterized as workaholics, the Japanese are finding increasing time to participate in a variety of leisure activities, including several sports imported from the West. Among the most popular are baseball, golf and skiing.

Japan adopted baseball from the United States as long ago as 1873. Today the game has so many players that public playing fields must be booked a month or two in advance. If teams are unable to get a slot during the normal hours, they may play as early as six a.m.

Baseball is also Japan's leading spectator sport, with 15 million people a year attending professional games. There are two major leagues, with six teams each, and great players acquire hero status (below, left).

More than a million and a half Japanese belong to golf clubs, where greens fees for members' guests can run as high as $100. Golf's popularity has partly to do with the fact that it is a convenient way to entertain business clients; not surprisingly, the players are almost always male.

Skiing, by contrast, is a family sport, and in a country as mountainous as Japan, it has no lack of devotees. Skiers outnumber golfers by almost 2 to 1.

fees are so high at most of the country's golf clubs, many Japanese get to play the game only when invited by friends or associates.

"THE DEVIL'S LANGUAGE"

Japanese has been called the "devil's language." The problem is not so much with spoken Japanese, which uses fewer sounds than any other major tongue, but with the way it is written. This glossary gives transliterations of some common expressions and then renders these into *kanji,* the system of writing in characters borrowed from China in the Fifth Century A.D.

There are about 50,000 characters in Japanese, some involving 40 different brushstrokes. Most of the 50,000 are rarely used, but a child is still required to master 1,850 of them, plus two phonetic syllabaries of 48 symbols each.

ENGLISH	TRANSLITERATION	JAPANESE
Good day!	*Konnichi wa!*	今日は
Good evening!	*Komban wa!*	今晩は
How are you?	*Ogenki desu ka?*	御元気ですか?
Fine.	*Genki desu.*	元気です。
Yes.	*Hai.*	はい
No.	*Iie.*	いいえ
Pardon me.	*Sumimasen.*	すみません。
I don't understand.	*Wakarimasen.*	判りません。(わかりません。)
Hello! (on the phone)	*Moshi, moshi!*	もしもし
Your name?	*O-namae wa?*	御名前は?
My name is . . .	*Watakushi wa . . . desu.*	私は………です。
How much is this?	*Kore wa ikura desu ka?*	これはいくらですか?
Where is the embassy?	*Taishikan wa doko desu ka?*	大使館はどこですか?
. . . restaurant?	*Ryoriya . . .?*	料理屋……?
. . . department store?	*Depato . . .?*	デパート……?
. . . bank?	*Ginko . . .?*	銀行……?
Please bring me water.	*O-mizu wo kudasai.*	お水をドさい。
. . . tea.	*O-cha. . . .*	お茶
. . . rice.	*Gohan. . . .*	御飯
Thank you.	*Domo arigato gozaimasu.*	どうもありがとうございます。
Thanks!	*Arigato!*	ありがとう
kitchen	*daidokoro*	台所
living room	*ima*	居間
theater	*gekijo*	劇場
taxi	*takushi*	タクシー
automobile	*jidosha*	自動車
airplane	*hikoki*	飛行機
subway	*chikatetsu*	地下鉄
today	*kyo*	今日
tomorrow	*ashita*	明日
day after tomorrow	*asatte*	あさって(明後日)

ial and other obligations. "My goal these days is to do everything I can for my family," one has avowed. "Give them a comfortable life in good surroundings. We all die sooner or later. I'm not especially bothered by the idea, but I want the satisfaction of knowing that I tried."

Equally important to Japan's production machine, although less visible because of their generally lower status, are the men and women who work on factory production lines. In the large, blue-chip companies these workers also have a virtual lifetime guarantee of employment. A spokesman for Nissan notes, "We don't use the term 'worker' any more. Everyone is a member of the Nissan family."

High-ranking members of a factory's family, such as long-entrenched foremen on quality-car production lines, may earn more than $20,000 a year — although that pay level is by no means common among workers lacking the imprimatur of a college degree. On this salary, perhaps with a modest boost from his parents or from his wife's family, a foreman may own a small, unpretentious house. Life may be made easier if his wife takes an income-supplementing part-time job in a shop or a small local plant or, if she attended a good high school, perhaps as an "office lady" whose principal functions are filing records and making tea.

The ordinary male factory hand enjoys few of the amenities of the foreman, even with the aid of a working wife. His domain is a cracker-box apartment no bigger than a one-car garage, which he shares with his wife and child. By day the bedding mats will simply be rolled and stored against the wall. A space heater or radiator will be turned on only in the coldest months, usually

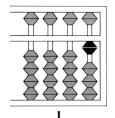 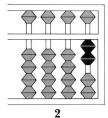 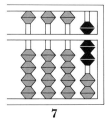 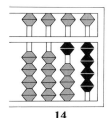 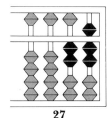 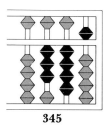

| 1 | 2 | 7 | 14 | 27 | 345 |

for just a few hours at a time to warm a corner where the family sits.

Bachelor men and the few unmarried women factory hands typically live in company barracks, which are clean and functional but often singularly graceless. One such barracks for men is Toyota's Third Ohbayashi Pleasant Breeze Dormitory. It houses more than 1,300 workers, who take breakfast and dinner together at a communal dining hall and watch television in a central social room.

Life in the Pleasant Breeze Dormitory, and others like it, is regimented in other ways, and so is life on the production line. Dormitory supervisors circulate among the men, reminding them to get up early, dress neatly and stay sober. On the job everyone wears the company uniform, complete with caps bearing colored markings that denote the nine ranks on the assembly line — two green stripes for the lowly seasonal worker, up to a black stripe for the exalted General Foreman.

Relatively few women work on the production lines — fewer still in the corporate suites — of Japan's larger companies. But increasingly, Japanese women want to have jobs rather than being, as they were in the past, confined to the home. Indeed, the role of women in Japan has been changing rapidly. Almost 40 per cent of the work force is made up of women — many of them employed as teachers, nurses or office workers. And many housewives are working at least part time in light industry, chiefly to boost the family income.

Despite this recently won independence and financial power, the notion has persisted that the woman's proper

place is in the home. Although according to recent polls more than 50 per cent of Japanese women under 30 years of age would like to have careers, they also want marriage and would, on balance, forgo the career for a home and the raising of children.

The appeal of homemaking has remained strong because Japanese housewives are not, contrary to worldwide impression, mincing, subservient cho-cho san who only follow their husbands' directives. They are instead — in part because their hard-working husbands are at home so little — tough-minded administrators who manage the household. They bring up the children and are known for pushing them relentlessly to study and achieve the high grades necessary for admission into a first-rate university — which in turn is the key to employment in a top corporation (Chapter 6).

Their power extends beyond the children to that pivot of control, the purse. A recent study by the Asahi newspaper corporation showed that eight out of 10 salarymen automatically turn over their paychecks to their wives, holding out an average of no more than $100 per month for a little bar-hopping or golf. The wives then take care of the entire budget — rental or mortgage payments, clothing, education, savings, vacations, appliance purchases, allowances and the rest. "I depend on her," says one sarariman, speaking for most of the rest, "and trust her to look after everything."

The housewife's daily round is almost as busy as her husband's. It often starts with several loads of wash — Japanese washing machines are generally

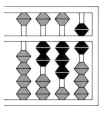 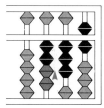

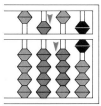 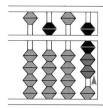

A simple problem, the addition of 272 to 236, is shown here. On the abacus, the Japanese customarily add from left to right, totaling the 100s, the 10s, then the units. The dark beads in the first drawing (top left) register 236. In the second drawing, two 100s have been moved up to total 400 on that rod. To add 70, the user cannot add seven 10s, because there are not enough beads on the 10s rod. Nor can the user add 100 and subtract 30, because all the 100s are up. The third sketch shows how to get 70: Add 500, subtract 430, (by moving four 100 beads and three 10 beads). This equals 70. Now the abacus beads total 506. In the last sketch, with two 1s added, the final answer becomes 508.

small and several loads are required to get everything clean. Washing is followed by another daily ritual, shopping for fresh produce at the local market. Afternoons are usually devoted to the children. When not actively overseeing home study sessions or running household affairs, the wife may spend her time in the company of other women, lunching or shopping with old school friends, or planning special activities with other parents at the school the children attend.

It is not strange that so many Japanese women continue to prefer home to the workplace. At home they are in charge. In offices and factories they suffer a degree of discrimination that would strike most Western women as medieval. Because many of the better-paying jobs are closed to them, women find it very difficult to advance into positions of real power. In all of Japan only 120,000 females hold any kind of managerial rank, mostly low. Many companies do not even interview women for executive positions.

Part of this stems from a system that is indeed feudal in its roots and remains so in some of its perceptions. A typical Japanese woman described her home training as beginning with her grandmother's admonition, "You're a girl, you bathe after the men." The balance of the message: to be a good girl and get married — preferably to someone selected by the parents. Approximately 60 per cent of marriages in Japan are still initiated by go-betweens — usually family friends who bring suitable couples together.

The maintenance of the traditional role also derives in part from a conviction among Japanese women that running a house and bringing up children constitute a sufficient challenge. Fur-

ther, considering the obstacles, the thought of doing full-scale battle in the man's arena does not seem all that attractive a choice. Indeed, the ferocious competition and enforced deferences on the business ladder are being evaluated by women with fast-growing skepticism. Said one woman who has watched Japan's new-wave generation of men centering their lives in their work, "I get to feeling pity for them."

Even those women who have launched careers have found that to some extent they must still meet demands the culture places on them. Dr. Akiko Matsui, an ear, nose and throat specialist married to another doctor, has successfully combined a thriving practice with the raising of two children. Medicine is one of the few vocations relatively open to Japan's two million professional women, primarily because the Japanese regard it as a skilled extension of the woman's so-called "natural nurturing" abilities. Nevertheless, Dr. Matsui recently recalled, "When I graduated from medical school in 1939, the same family

friend who had encouraged me to become a doctor congratulated me and then said, 'Now go home and get the milk started' — meaning, forget medicine and have a baby." Interestingly, Dr. Matsui might well have given up her profession had the War not called her husband away and created an urgent need for doctors at home.

She did quit when he came back after the War. For the next 10 years she stayed home to have a daughter and son, and to manage the house. Only occasionally did she assist her husband in surgery. But in the late 1950s, with both children in school, she went back into practice, ministering — with characteristic Japanese energy — to about 100 patients a day. For Dr. Matsui it has seemed entirely natural to keep on doing the housework while carrying out her professional responsibilities, and she clearly has handled her demanding multiple roles with grace and satisfaction. Indeed her major concern has been today's female medical-school graduates. To her dismay a great many of them have taken their degrees as in-

Drinking tea on his bed, an employee of Japan's leading tire company makes the most of his cramped quarters in one of the firm's bachelor dormitories. The workers buy in company stores, marry in company wedding halls and vacation at company resorts.

tellectual honor badges and have then married, with no desire or intent ever to practice medicine.

More rebellious and outspokenly critical of the system, yet ultimately as successful in conforming, has been Tomoko, a television producer. Tomoko herself admits that for a woman to have gotten such a job in Japan was "like winning a lottery." And indeed, without an extraordinary amount of luck — plus innate talent and drive — the only way a Japanese woman can get near a television camera is to be a *"Hai-hai* girl," who stands prettily next to the all-knowing male newscaster chirping *"Hai-hai!"* ("Yes-yes!") at his pronouncements.

That was never going to be for Tomoko, who started saying "No-no!" to some cherished Japanese conventions a long time ago. In college she fell in love with a Japanese man whom she met in German class. Her mother, Tomoko recently recalled, became "very worked up" that the family had not been allowed a hand in arranging her marriage. But Tomoko calmly announced she would marry the man of her choice — which she did.

Then it was his turn for some sur-

prises. "He thought his woman would clean the house for him every day," she remembers, "but I'm not the type. I didn't follow orders. Little by little he began doing it himself. He was the one who prepared all the baby food when we were weaning our son."

She also refused to play other roles that the Japanese expect of wives and mothers. "We intended to have another child," she points out, "but I became too tied down at work." And for their one child, a boy, she has been anything but the usual Japanese *kyoiku mama,* or "education mamma." "I don't dote on him," she says. "I have no intention of pushing him into a college-prep course. His current ambition is to become a professional baseball player. If he really should turn out to have the needed talent for it, I wouldn't stand in his way. I want him to develop the ability to think for himself, decide for himself. And I suppose I want him to end up married to a complete woman."

Despite this iconoclastic toughness, she has continued to like and admire her husband, who turned out to be strong in a gentle way, and supportive. When Tomoko was striving to land the

producer's job, he was entirely on her side, believing that a qualified woman never should allow herself to "end up just pouring tea for the men." She did not, although the road has not been easy. "When I joined the Osaka studio," she recently recounted, "you just trailed after an experienced producer and learned by imitating him." She mastered the profession quickly and well — but discovered just as fast "what a feudalistic place ours is. They don't do a thing to help a woman develop her abilities."

Nor have they done anything to open the way toward any choice assignments. Although Tomoko has long coveted a serious news show, she has become resigned to the fact that "women are stuck with the ordinary little daily programs." These are the home-cooking and crafts shows, derisively called "tea and flowers" programs — "the ones the men don't want." She is reluctant to assume an executive role. "I've avoided taking administrative positions," she says. "As an administrator you're a tool. You have to change your personality, and the tensions mount. All the men seem eager to go that route. But soon they look awfully haggard and worn."

Thus the rebel has taken comfort from her realistic assessment of the pros and cons of a man's world that is so highly resistant to internal change — although the external changes in modern Japan increase at an exponential rate. "I'm doing my work for the studio peacefully," she sums up, sounding very much like any factory hand or *sarariman,* "and I don't really want to leave it, for better or for worse. To want to be like a man is incredibly irresponsible. To remain a woman, and still be able to raise the quality of life for the rest — this is what I want to do." ☐

THE SARARIMAN

Climbing the corporate ladder is challenge enough in the Western world, but it is an even greater one in Japan. Hideo Onishi is among those lucky few who are making it to the top. At 38, he is responsible for sales and development of video disk players and software in a division of one of the world's largest makers of consumer electronic goods, Matsushita. He is a university graduate and speaks fluent English, polished when he worked in Canada and the U.S. (he still likes being called by his American nickname, Hank). He enjoys all the privileges of an executive, including a generous expense account and the respect that comes with rank. Moreover, he has an attractive house in an Osaka suburb and a car in which to drive to work.

As the price for his success, Onishi must give himself 100 per cent to the company. His devotion brings him to the office most Saturdays and requires him to spend long days on the job, and often long evenings as well, entertaining clients. His wife accepts this; she sees her job as running the household and raising their two daughters.

Participating in the morning ritual at Matsushita Electric, manager Onishi listens to the company creed. His badge proclaims Matsushita's goal — to increase productivity 10 per cent.

After breakfasting on scrambled eggs and toast, Hideo Onishi bids farewell to his family as he sets off for work. He leaves at 6:30 each morning to reach the office by 7:15.

At an afternoon meeting, Onishi
reviews plans for a new video disk
player with engineers from Technics, a
division of Matsushita. This was
one of eight meetings he attended
before leaving the office at 7 p.m.

Surrounded by uniformed assembly-
line workers, Onishi and fellow
managers eat in the company cafeteria.
"They believe in peace, brotherhood —
and market share," one wag said of
Matsushita's democratic ways.

Bowing deeply, Onishi and a colleague say good-by to a client. Such formalities are a regular part of Japanese business life.

Onishi (in blue-gray suit) takes visiting executives out for dinner at Osaka's finest restaurant on his expense account. Food and drinks, with entertainment provided by geisha, came to $300 a person.

After dinner, Onishi and his guests stop at a hostess bar. Such relaxation away from the formalities of the office is viewed by Japanese businessmen as enhancing understanding and the free exchange of ideas.

In his Sunday role as a family man,
Onishi joins his wife, Noriko, and their
two daughters on a ride at an
amusement park near their home.

40

Onishi and family get set for a Wild West photograph. In addition to managing the household, Noriko is active in the parent-teacher association of her daughters' school.

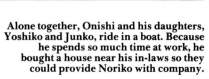

Alone together, Onishi and his daughters, Yoshiko and Junko, ride in a boat. Because he spends so much time at work, he bought a house near his in-laws so they could provide Noriko with company.

41

Following along behind his hand plow, a farmer cultivates a garden plot. On his feet are *jikatabi*, cloven, stocking-like footwear with rubber soles. The tight-clinging *jikatabi* are regularly worn by farmers and workers.

THE BEAUTIFUL, DANGEROUS LAND

Visitors arriving in Japan today by jet aircraft miss a sight that drew gasps from earlier travelers nearing Tokyo by ship — the vista of Mount Fuji rising snow-capped and majestic on the horizon. This introduction to Japan was not only impressive but also peculiarly fitting, because Mount Fuji can stand as the epitome of elemental Japan, a symbol of the entire land.

Towering to 12,389 feet, Mount Fuji is first of all a reminder that Japan is an exceedingly mountainous nation. All four of the main islands — from Kyushu and Shikoku in the south through Honshu to Hokkaido in the north — are bisected and dominated by mountain ranges. Many of these are breathtakingly lovely, their precipitous, tree-clad flanks diving into deep valleys with swift streams, shimmering lakes and occasional emerald fields. The largest of the islands, Honshu, is famous for its mountain vistas, one craggy range visible behind another until the most distant peaks vanish in the moisture-laden blue-gray haze that lends a uniquely Japanese softness to such landscapes. Its many mountains help make Japan one of the most beautiful countries on earth.

But this beauty has its penalties. It is Japan's deeply corrugated, largely uninhabitable mountains — which cover about 71 per cent of the land area — that make the small segments of habitable flatland so overcrowded. Most of the people, as well as the country's industries and farms, are cramped into the narrow alluvial basins and plains that lie at the foot of the islands' mountainous interiors. Japan's largest metropolitan area, the Tokyo-Yokohama megalopolis, contains no fewer than 27 major and minor cities, and the Nagoya complex has about 20. These two regions, along with the Kobe-Kyoto-Osaka industrial area, occupy southeastern Honshu's three main coastal basins. Among them they house and employ more than 50 million people, nearly half of Japan's entire population. Together they form a 320-mile-long industrial corridor that for sheer crowdedness has few equals anywhere.

Japan's many mountain ranges also severely limit the areas suitable for agriculture. Only 16 per cent of the land is arable, and the space available for crops is further reduced by encroaching suburbs. Yet even today the farmers produce 72 per cent of all the agricultural foodstuffs the Japanese consume, including 90 per cent of the fruit. These farmers, with a big assist from Japan's hardworking fishermen, have provided much of the needed protein as well. They have done so through dedicated, unrelieved toil that verges on the heroic. That Japan's farmers, despite spreading industries and a growing population, continue to produce most of what their fellow citizens eat is almost as miraculous as the huge postwar expansion of the nation's industries.

The seaborne traveler's distant

2

glimpse of Mount Fuji's symmetrical volcanic cone was also a dramatic reminder of Japan's geological origins and a suitable warning of the seismic violence that afflicts the nation. No other densely populated, industrialized country lives in such immediate and mortal peril from volcanic eruptions and earthquakes. The four main islands and about 3,000 smaller ones that constitute Japan were thrust up from the Pacific seabed through crustal folding and vulcanism in recent geologic time, and the immense subterranean forces that created them remain awe-

somely alive. Japan is shaken by more than 1,000 perceptible tremors annually, and every few years a serious quake occurs somewhere in the country, destroying buildings and killing people.

The cause of this intense seismic activity can be traced to slow but implacable movements in the earth's crust. According to the modern geological theory of plate tectonics, the planet's rigid outer shell, the lithosphere, consists of gigantic plates that move ponderously about in response to forces generated within the molten interior of the earth. Three of these plates crunch

into one another off the shores of Japan. The massive 8,000-mile-wide Pacific Plate is being forced beneath the Eurasian Plate along the coast of northeastern Honshu, while the smaller Philippine Plate grinds against the Eurasian Plate along southern Honshu, Shikoku and Kyushu.

These titanic collisions created Japan's sharply upthrust mountains over a period of millions of years, and they are still going on. Continual small adjustments between the plates cause the teacup-rattling tremors that are a part of Japanese daily life. At the same time,

friction between the plates forces magma up through fissures in the subterranean rock to cause volcanic eruptions. About a quarter of Japan's 192 volcanic peaks have spewed molten lava and ash during the nation's recorded history, and many remain active to this day. Massive rearrangements of the rock masses beneath Japan produce the nation's big quakes.

They can be catastrophic. A major quake in June 1948, measuring a whopping 7.3 on the Richter scale, virtually demolished the small city of Fukui in western Honshu. Far worse was the great quake that struck Tokyo and Yokohama on September 1, 1923. That earthquake, the most destructive in Japan's recorded history, began about noon on a busy Saturday with a series of violent shocks produced by a rupture in the earth under nearby Sagami Bay. The area's wooden houses soon looked, according to one observer, "as if they had been battered by a giant flail."

Charcoal cookstoves, red-hot for the lunch hour, turned the debris into a conflagration. In the capital's central wards, two great walls of fire pushed terrified mobs of people toward the Sumida River. There the converging crowds were trapped. Many of the victims drowned in the river, many more were incinerated. In all, 130,000 people perished, as many as were killed by the atomic bomb that leveled Hiroshima in 1945.

Should an earthquake of similar intensity rock the Tokyo-Yokohama area today, the effects might well be worse. Many homes employ kerosene for heating and bottled gas for cooking, both vastly more flammable than charcoal. The Japanese do what they can to be ready. Engineers working with earthquake scientists have come up with designs for buildings that theoretically will not collapse during a quake. Strict zoning laws mandate that all tall structures built in downtown areas conform to such designs. Earthquake drills in schools and offices are frequent. Many homes have survival kits containing food and medicines, and fire extinguishers are everywhere, even in taxicabs. But the experts admit that another quake of the magnitude of the one in 1923 might topple thousands of structures and kill as many as half a million people.

Earthquakes off Japan's coast or volcanic eruptions in or near the sea can cause another destructive phenomenon — huge sea waves, often miscalled tidal waves. These may reach as much as 100 feet in height and slam ashore with devastating force. So familiar are such waves in Japan that scientists all over the world know them by their Japanese name, tsunami.

The region most vulnerable to tsunamis is the northeast coast of Honshu, where the collision of the Pacific and Eurasian Plates makes offshore quakes common. But they can happen elsewhere. A tsunami struck Honshu's northwest coast in May of 1983 after an earthquake measuring 7.7 on the Richter scale rocked the floor of the Sea of Japan. More than a hundred people perished in the monstrous wave or in the destruction caused onshore by the quake itself. Included were 13 schoolchildren, members of a class that was just beginning a beach picnic when the tsunami hurtled in. A local fisherman saved some of the children but recalled in horror seeing others being carried out to sea.

There is yet another violent phenomenon that regularly threatens Japan — the typhoon (from the Chinese *taai fung,* or "great wind"). These cyclonic storms roar into Japan's coastal areas from the warm seas to the south. Resembling the hurricanes that batter the Southeastern United States, they arrive in late summer and early autumn, wreaking severe damage on crops. A half dozen typhoons pass over or near Japan every season, some of them taking a heavy toll in lives and property along the densely populated coasts.

In Japan, nature can be as serene as it is wrathful. Some of the country's loveliest spots lie on the southernmost main island of Kyushu. Blessed with a subtropical climate and a coastline indented by peaceful bays and inlets, it is a favored vacation spot for city dwellers from farther north. A visitor beginning a tour of Japan there would find the handsome Kyushu Range, which runs down the island's spine and gives way to narrow coastal flatlands where old-fashioned farming villages are surrounded by patchworks of small green fields and orchards.

Even in this seeming paradise, however, there are dangers, for Kyushu also has several of Japan's most awesome volcanoes. Mile-high Mount Aso has five separate cones contained within a crater 15 miles long and 10 miles wide, the world's largest. Inside the crater is a fuming vent that has spewed molten lava in paroxysmal blasts more than 100 times since 796 A.D., when the first eruption was recorded.

Mount Aso is matched in height by Mount Kirishima to the south. Farther south, on a peninsula that juts into Kagoshima Bay, is another active volcano, Mount Sakurajima, 3,668 feet high, and on Kyushu's western coast rises the bulk of 4,460-foot Mount Unzen. This impressive cone has erupted only five times since its first recorded blast in the

A rice paddy glows with the reflected light of sunset in the Japanese Alps, part of a mountain chain that bisects the largest of the four main islands, Honshu.

A PASSION
FOR HOT WATER

Deep beneath the volcanic chain of islands that is Japan, water is heated by internal fires. From this caldron of geothermal activity come the steam and springs that rise in the country's 1,600 spas.

Bathing in hot springs — which can be a social occasion in Japan — follows a closely prescribed ritual. For the most part, the sexes use segregated pools. Before entering, the bather washes and rinses off carefully, then enters the hot water (ideal temperature: around 110° F.) and remains immersed as long as possible before emerging to dry off with a towel.

Nowhere is the hot-spring business bigger than in Beppu, about a one-hour jet flight southwest from Tokyo. A city of only 140,000, it annually attracts almost 12 million tourists to its waters. Every 24 hours, more than 10 million gallons of scalding water gush forth from belowground, some of it close to boiling.

"Properly taken," says one official of Beppu's Research Institute of Balneotherapeutics, a scientific center devoted to the study of therapeutic uses of baths, "a dip in a hot spring promotes circulation, stimulates hormone glands." If the Japanese needed any reason for their love affair with hot water, that would be enough.

At Takaragawa Hot Springs, north of Tokyo, male bathers relax alongside a mountain stream rushing through the village, after a dip in the springs situated under a shed roof.

Clouds of steam rise over the old
part of Beppu. The town sits on more
than 4,000 geothermal sources.

Beppu's "Bloody Pond Hell," which gets its red color from iron oxide in the water, has a surface temperature of close to 212° F. — almost boiling, and much too hot for bathers.

At a spa on the Izu Peninsula two women soak in a 22-karat gold tub shaped like a Chinese phoenix. The management charges a special fee for every five minutes' use of this tub.

Toweled headbands protecting their eyes from perspiration, two men sweat in a Beppu mud bath. One hotel even offers a coffee bath: The bather is buried to the neck in crunched coffee beans heated by an infusion of spring water.

Faces protected from the sun, women lie buried in Beppu's volcanic sand, warmed by thermal springs beneath.

Mount Sakurajima's Minamidake cone in southern Kyushu sends a churning cloud of ash aloft in an eruption. Japan is home to one tenth of the earth's active volcanoes.

year 860, but the huge explosion of 1792 caused 14,000 deaths.

Sakurajima, by contrast, shakes and shudders frequently (Minamidake, one of its three cones, is one of the world's most active volcanoes), but in recent centuries it has produced few fatal eruptions. The neighboring people over the centuries have learned to live with their mountain. The lava and ash produced by the large eruption of 1914 caused much damage but took few lives; the villagers nearby had prudently moved a safe distance away when preliminary rumblings began. Today Sakurajima bears a cheerful, domesticated aspect; neat groves of citrus trees dot its lower slopes.

Kyushu's generally benign climate allows three growing seasons a year in some areas. On the island's fertile coastal flatlands the people raise cattle as well as rice and a wide variety of vegetables and fruits. Much of Kyushu seems to belong to a bucolic, preindustrial Japan. Except for the northern section of the island, where the fire-breathing steel mills of Kitakyushu and the shipyards and factories of Nagasaki are located, it appears an ancient land, which indeed it is.

Kyushu was the cradle of Japanese civilization, the inviting place where the forebears of today's Japanese first came ashore after navigating the Korea Strait from the Asian mainland (Chapter 3). It was from Kyushu, according to Japanese legend, that the first Emperor, Jimmu, started out on his conquest of the rest of Japan.

The Emperor would have had little trouble crossing the Shimonoseki Strait, which divides Kyushu from Honshu; it is less than a mile across. Under it today dive railroad tunnels for the long-distance bullet trains that

Dazed survivors of the 1948 Fukui earthquake — which measured 7.3 on the Richter scale — survey the damage to their city. More than 3,500 people died, many of them in fires that swept through the wreckage of their homes.

2

speed toward Tokyo along the eastern coast of sea horse-shaped Honshu. The southern portion of Honshu, like every other part of Japan, has its own spine of mountains and narrow coastal plains, and around Kobe there are a surprising number of small cattle farms. From these come some of the superb prime steaks that Western-oriented Japanese businessmen favor. One secret of the beef's succulence is that the steers are encouraged to drink large quantities of beer. Some farmers also give their pampered animals regular massages, which help lend tenderness and marbling to the meat.

The southern coast of Honshu borders on the nearly landlocked body of water called the Inland Sea. Confined on the south by the smallest of the main islands, Shikoku, this lakelike arm of the Pacific is dotted with hundreds of verdant islets, many so small as to be uninhabited, others sheltering ancient fishing villages and religious shrines. "Wherever one turns," wrote an enthusiastic visitor, "there is a wide and restful view."

For all its placid mien, the Inland Sea, 40 miles across at its widest, is a busy thoroughfare. Ferries ply between Shikoku and Honshu, as do cargo ships carrying the products of Shikoku's rich, intensively farmed lowlands — rice, wheat and barley as well as mandarin oranges, persimmons, peaches, grapes and all manner of vegetables grown on its sunny southern shore. Also crossing the Inland Sea are large freighters, colliers and tankers heading to and from the Kobe-Kyoto-Osaka industrial complex, located where the Honshu sea horse's tail joins the body.

Northeast of Kyoto and nearby Nagoya are Honshu's (and the country's) highest mountain ranges, including

several known collectively as the Japanese Alps. The mountains continue into northern Honshu, neatly dividing the island in two. The eastern half, which faces the Pacific, is by far the more populous, having most of the nation's largest cities. The other half is less familiar to most outsiders and even to a majority of Japanese themselves. It is known somewhat disparagingly as Ura Nihon, the "Backside of Japan."

This northwestern coast of Honshu boasts several good-sized cities — Toyama, Niigata, Akita — but generally it is more rural than the eastern face of the island. There is a certain wildness to the area, exemplified by extraordinary winter snowfalls that do not so much blanket the region as bury it. Cold winds blowing down from Siberia and picking up moisture over the Sea of Japan release such huge amounts of snow that from December to April only the railroad tracks are plowed out. Highways are closed, and villagers get about through streets they have converted into snow tunnels. For its latitude — roughly equivalent to that of southern Spain — western Honshu, where drifts in the mountains can be as much as

15 feet deep, is surely the snowiest place on the globe.

The northernmost main island, Hokkaido, has a similar rural quality. It is the closest thing Japan has to a frontier area. Not until the late 19th Century did the central government in Tokyo set about colonizing the island, partly to open new agricultural areas, partly to discourage any ideas the Russian Tsar might have had of adding Hokkaido to his Far Eastern realm.

The colonization made inroads on the wilderness, but much remains. Brown bears still roam the forests. Pristine lakes and impressive stands of primeval spruce and fir are protected in four national parks, as are volcanic areas where hot springs bubble and steam to the surface. Despite the neat farms and the island's flourishing ski resorts, Hokkaido retains the feel of a northern outpost. It reminded one visiting American writer of "Tasmania, Patagonia, Scandinavia, Alaska — nothing between here and the Pole."

The farms of Hokkaido also have a different feel and look from those on the more southerly islands. When Hokkaido was being colonized roughly a

An Ainu chief warms himself before a fire in a reed hut on Hokkaido. The Ainu, Japan's aboriginal inhabitants, claim to have been discriminated against by the Japanese and are seeking to recover their ethnic identity.

century ago, the Tokyo government invited a number of U.S. farm experts to help shape the new land. One disconcerting result is that many farms have large, red, American-style barns and tall silos, giving the landscape a curious resemblance to the valleys of rural Pennsylvania. Hokkaido's farms, which average 12.5 acres each, are also larger than the Japanese norm. Although some cultivate the nation's staple grain, rice, others produce onions, potatoes, beans, oats and wheat. Hokkaido is also Japan's primary producer of milk and other dairy products.

The principal losers in the development of Hokkaido were the Ainu, a mysterious people who had made the island their last refuge from Japanese encroachment. The Ainu, most scholars agree, inhabited Japan long before the Asian ancestors of the Japanese ar-

rived, but who the Ainu are or where they came from remains unknown. Their comparatively round eyes with curling lashes and their thick, wavy hair would seem to indicate that they must be at least remotely a Caucasoid people who migrated east instead of west millennia ago. Archeological evidence suggests that their tenure in Japan dates back to 5000 B.C.

Whatever their origins, the Ainu were being pushed northward out of Honshu by the far more numerous Japanese as early as the Eighth Century A.D. Today they are a vanishing people; only 15,000 to 18,000 can still claim Ainu heritage, and perhaps only 300 have full-blood Ainu ancestry.

For many years the Japanese majority has forced the Ainu to take Japanese names and to learn the Japanese language in school. As a result of such

forced Japanization, the ancient Ainu language and culture have fast been disappearing — although a recently born Ainu Liberation Movement may help preserve some of that cultural heritage. One pressing task is to write down a long folk epic called the *Yukar*, which has been passed on orally from generation to generation. None of the Ainu elders today are able to recite the entire poem, but among them much of the epic might be recalled and reconstructed.

Another liberation movement has been trying to improve the lot of Japan's two million other outcasts who are euphemistically known as *burakumin*, or "village people." The old name for them was *eta*, meaning "full of filth," and for centuries they have been considered untouchable, like the people of the lowest caste in India. The

2

source of this stigma may be traceable to Buddhism, which forbade the eating or touching of meat and judged those who dealt with blood and death, such as butchers, leatherworkers and grave-diggers, to be unclean. The *burakumin*, who performed these tasks, were forced to live in segregated communities and, although ethnically Japanese, have long been discriminated against in jobs and education.

The prejudice lingers. The profession of marriage detective flourishes in Japan largely because families feel it essential to discover whether a prospective son- or daughter-in-law has any trace of *burakumin* ancestry. The *burakumin*, however, possess all the legal rights of Japanese citizens, and their liberation movement appears to be making progress in bringing to an end the various forms of discrimination, both overt and subtle, from which they have suffered.

Many *burakumin* are indeed village people — workers and farmers in Japan's agricultural areas — and, along with all of the nation's rural people, they have begun to benefit from the general postwar upsurge in the economy, and from handsome government crop subsidies. The farm families of Japan today can boast incomes that approach those of white-collar workers.

This is a happy change from the past. For centuries Japan's farmers were the backbone of the nation — and were gouged mercilessly by the feudal tax collectors. As an old saying put it, "Peasants should not be allowed to die, nor yet to live." Many tenant farmers worked for wealthy — and, in modern times, often absentee — landlords.

The postwar Allied Occupation forced landowners to sell most or all of their holdings to farm workers at ab-

Nature distilled, the perfectly scaled garden of the 16th Century Katsura Palace in Kyoto features tiny islands planted with exquisitely trained trees. The stone lantern perches on what is meant to evoke a stretch of rocky coast.

Clouds of steam rise over the old part of Beppu. The town sits on more than 4,000 geothermal sources.

48

Silhouetted in morning light, a
Buddhist priest contemplates the
colors of autumn. The Japanese make
much of the seasons; ancient verses
regularly refer to them, though often
obliquely — grasshoppers and wild
geese, for example, suggesting fall.

surdly low prices. Overnight Japanese farming villages became communities of farmer-owners, whose land would increase remarkably in value as real-estate prices soared all over Japan. Some families sold out and took the profit, but many more stayed on the land, in part at least because their crops brought better prices than ever before. By one recent count, Japan still had about 4.6 million farm households, representing 12.8 per cent of the population. In few other industrialized nations is such a large proportion of the people engaged in agriculture.

These statistics are somewhat misleading, however, because only about 580,000 of the farm households derive their entire incomes from farming. The traditional farm family of Japan — like those in parts of Europe — was once a wholly cohesive unit with several generations living and working together. Today several generations may live under the same roof, but increasingly one or more of the family members bring in extra income by commuting to an office or factory job in a nearby city. The chief commuter is generally the young husband and father. He is often joined by his sons and daughters when they become old enough to hold jobs.

This leaves the farm to be worked, on weekdays at least, by the older generation, the grandfather and grandmother, and by the daughter-in-law. In some families the daughter-in-law is relegated to the wholly unenviable Cinderella role of lighting the day's first fire and scrubbing the floors as well as working long hours in the fields.

In recent years Japan's women's liberation movement has prompted government concern for the health and well-being of all the nation's farm women, old and young, who are forced to work desperately hard to keep the family acreage in profitable operation. The Ministry of Labor has established a Women's and Young Workers' Bureau to study the problems of farm life in modern Japan. In addition, Women's Associations have sprung up in many rural areas; they have been holding seminars that examine the struggles farm women face and that suggest ways of improving farms and reducing the domestic workload.

The status of the once commonly overworked daughter-in-law has also changed, for quite practical reasons. The availability of city jobs for women

has made it difficult for young farmers to attract wives — and to keep them down on the farm. The independent young daughter-in-law of today is less likely to be intimidated and exploited by a domineering mother-in-law.

Whatever the family arrangement, the combination of farm and outside income has provided many rural families with amenities and luxuries undreamed of in once-impoverished rural Japan. A recent study revealed that 17 of the 23 families in one small village had at least one automobile, and almost all had automatic rice cookers, refrigerators, washing machines and color television sets — all quite new.

According to this same study, the farm family's diet has altered dramatically, too. Fish and meat, luxuries not long ago, have become regular fare. And the farmhouses themselves have changed. Kitchens where smoke curled up from an open hearth to find its way out through the roof have become stainless-steel and formica wonders with strip lighting and butane-fueled gas ranges. All-glass aluminum-framed sliding doors have been substituted for the old wooden ones. And thatched roofs have been largely replaced by tile.

One thing that has changed little so far is the pattern of land use in rural areas. As in many parts of Europe, the farmers cluster their dwellings in small communities, which are encircled by the villagers' cultivated plots. What has no parallel in Europe or America is the size of these plots. By any standard they are astonishingly small. As the 1980s began, there were only 13.3 million acres under cultivation in all of Japan, and the size of the average farm — even including Hokkaido's bigger spreads — was a tiny 2.9 acres.

Small as they are, most Japanese

Undaunted by rain, Japanese view the
cherry blossoms in a Tokyo park.
The brief season of the scentless
blossoms is cause for merriment, and
revelers often party beneath the
boughs. But thoughts of mortality
intrude soon after, when the petals fall.

farms are subdivided into many fields dispersed across the countryside. Some will usually be wet fields for growing rice, some dry fields for vegetables or other grains. Many farmers also own upland plots suitable for orchards.

This seemingly chaotic system is the child of a long history of buying, renting, bartering and inheriting, but it has its merits. Although inefficient, it is equitable, giving virtually everyone in the village some rich land — and some that is not so good. What makes it all work is the extraordinary amount of labor Japanese farm people expend on their small, scattered fields and the numbers of people still engaged in agriculture. More than five times as many workers cultivate any given square mile of farmland as in Germany, which has long been known for its intensive agriculture. The Japanese tend their plots, one observer has noted, "more like gardens than farm fields." The rice yield per acre in Japan is two to four times that found in Southeast Asia.

Abundant rain — up to 110 inches a year in some areas — and a generally mild climate help Japan's farmers attain such yields. And machinery helps, too. Japan's farmers have spent heavily to mechanize rice production within the limits of their small fields. A generation ago, seedlings could only be planted by hand, cluster by cluster, as a recruited force of family and neighbors waded through the paddies, setting out the plants with military precision. Today a farmer can rent or buy a motorized planter that neatly sets out trays of seedlings. Virtually every other aspect of rice cultivation has been changed by technology. A lightweight tilling machine has replaced the oxdrawn plow; herbicides have eliminated weeding; chemicals have been substituted for more laborious fertilizing methods; and harvesting is done by machine, with dryers and hullers finishing the grain for market. Only the interim stacking of rice sheaves in the fields in neat, artistic patterns that differ from region to region is still of necessity a hand process.

An automatic rice planter makes a once-backbreaking chore easy. All the operator need do is guide the machine as a mechanical belt removes seedlings from a tray and inserts the roots gently in the mud. Such planters are now common throughout Japan.

A rice-growing hamlet nestled in a valley near Kyoto suggests the timeless nature of Japan's countryside. As in so many other agricultural areas of this mountainous nation, forested slopes rise up from the paddies to constitute a realm of their own.

2

The changes in rice production have meant far greater reward for fewer hours expended — exactly what today's part-time farmers need. One study published in 1978 found that 70 years before, an acre of rice took 90 to 100 days to ready for market, and a harvest of fifteen 132-pound bales was a good one. In the 1950s the same acre required 50 to 60 days' labor and — thanks to improved rice varieties, fertilizers and pest control — yielded 20 bales. By the time the study was made, only 30 to 35 days of work were required to produce 25 bales.

Advances in farming techniques and the growth of commuting — along with the coming of the telephone and the ubiquity of television — have brought changes in the life of the farm village, or *buraku*. Many of the ties of neighborliness that united farm hamlets have weakened. Formerly, every household in a village sent someone to help with the annual repair of the local roads. Today the job is usually done by the local government. Weddings, once great festive occasions held at the house of the groom, are now often held at wedding halls, at considerable expense and with less conviviality. Funerals, which once required men of the *buraku* to build the funeral pyre themselves and reduce the corpse to ashes, have been handed over to undertakers. Religious celebrations at local shrines stand in danger of becoming dull: The young men no longer have enough time to practice the rituals that are associated with these festivals.

But what modern ways have pulled apart, the processes of farming can pull back together — particularly the ancient necessities of rice farming. Rice cultivation still depends on the successful management of intricate communal irrigation systems. "The rice producer has no choice but to work in concert with others who cultivate land in which his village lies," wrote anthropologist and Japan expert Robert Smith. "He cannot make arbitrary decisions, nor can he decide independently of his neighbors when to take in water, raise or lower the levels in his fields, and when to drain them."

Some of Japan's farm villages, not surprisingly, are attracting a wholly new sort of resident — city workers desperate to escape the cramped quarters and bewildering crowds of Japan's large urban areas. Rural hamlets that are close enough to the workers' jobs are seeing more and more refugees from the *rasshu-awa* (rush hour).

This looming suburbanization of some farm areas may in time reduce the acreage devoted to crops, forcing Japan to import a greater percentage of its food than it has in the past. So may the flight of the children of farm families to jobs in the nearest city, or even to the neon lure of Tokyo.

That farm villages and farm families will not disappear seems assured, however — for some powerful political reasons. Because of the way electoral districts have been drawn, rural regions send a disproportionate number of representatives to the Japanese parliament, or Diet. The Liberal Democratic Party, which has dominated the Diet through most of the postwar era, derives a great deal of its strength from these outlying precincts. In order to hold on to its political control of the countryside, the LDP has maintained agricultural price supports that particularly favor rice growers. So long as this aid continues, it seems safe to say that rural Japan will keep much of its ancient charm and beauty. □

Braving a Hokkaido snowstorm with an oilpaper umbrella, a woman walks toward the ice-encrusted sea. Hokkaido is Japan's second-largest island, but because of its chilly climate and poor soil, it has less than 5 per cent of the nation's population of 120 million.

On a lucky August day, Ine fishermen haul a swordfish aboard. In addition, they caught 1,500 yellowtail — a good catch in a month usually plagued by bad currents and typhoons.

A COOPERATIVE LIVELIHOOD FROM THE SEA

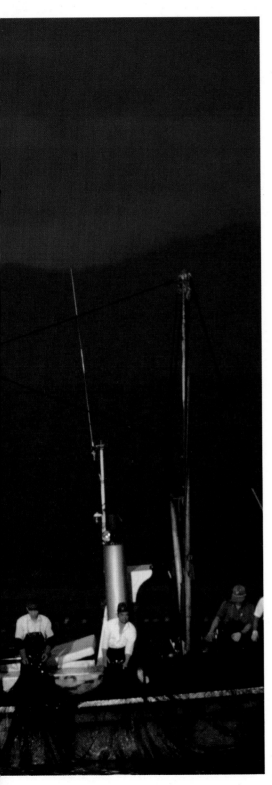

A sea-girt nation, Japan has long depended on fish as a major source of protein. Today its fishing industry, the world's most successful in terms of annual catch, is almost completely organized on a cooperative basis; 90 per cent of the catch is hauled in by men who belong to one of the country's 4,400 fishing co-ops.

The average co-op is small. The fishermen shown on these pages—all from the village of Ine on Wakasa Bay, about 95 miles northwest of Kyoto—belong to one that draws its 330 members from Ine and the surrounding area. A few of the fishermen own their boats, but the majority work on salary (about $700 a month).

Life for the men is hard. Most of them go out at dawn each day and work until dark before returning with their catch. Those using the co-op's largest boat, a 20-ton vessel, may stay out for as long as four months, fishing off Hokkaido for sardines, their most profitable catch.

Common interest and common goals make for a tight-knit community. In addition to organizing and marketing the catch, the co-op, which is tax-exempt and subsidized by the government, provides hospitals and clinics, low-cost vacation houses, banking and other benefits for its members. To supplement the income from fishing, many of the women work; a few engage in an Ine specialty, weaving lavish cloth for kimonos and the wide sashes worn with them.

As the fishermen get older, they tend to leave Ine and other such ports to search for easier factory jobs in nearby cities. Their children often find that they prefer life in the city to that of a village. The government and the co-ops, already concerned that the deep-sea catch is tapering off because of the 200-mile offshore limit most of the world's coastal zones now enforce, are increasing their financial incentives to keep fishermen on the boats and in the coastal villages—or to lure them back.

Operating three miles offshore, a crew pulls up its net. The boat can hold more than 20 tons of fish.

Ashore, the men repair nets. They work systematically, a section at a time; no one starts on the next section until each has finished mending his part.

Fisherman's wife Sakae Okuno hangs squid out on her clothes rack to dry for later consumption. Co-op families are allowed first pick of the day's catch, and what they take is charged to their monthly account.

Backed by steep hills, Ine hugs the shore of Wakasa Bay. The houses, quite large for Japan, include a living room, kitchen, bathroom, foyer, several bedrooms and a berth underneath for mooring boats. Some homeowners use part of their berths for cultivating fish — usually yellowtail.

At a table laden with raw and grilled fish, pickled cucumber and radish, rice, an omelette, tomatoes and sake, co-op fisherman Toru Hiraoka describes a bombing attack American planes made on Wakasa Bay during World War II, as his wife listens.

After a long day aboard his vessel, Hisao Sado, the co-op head, relaxes in his tub. The spigot next to the tub is for rinsing off before the actual bath.

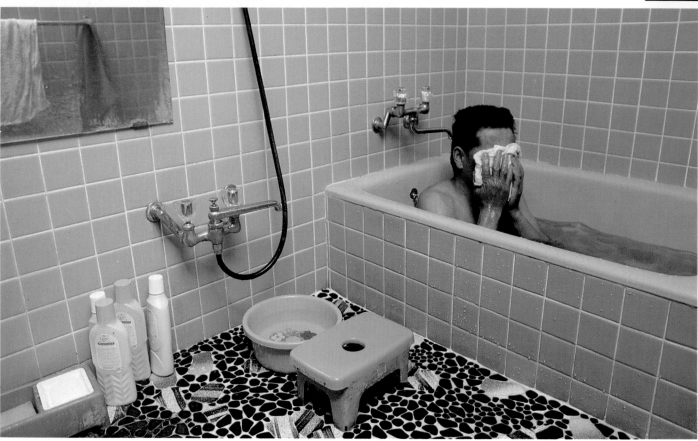

Refreshed by his bath, Sado sips tea
in the room in his house where
offerings are made to his family's
ancestors. The scroll on the wall
behind him shows a beaming
fisherman with a fish on his hook.

To supplement its fish diet, every family grows vegetables on a small piece of land like this hillside patch. The family-owned gardens, usually about a five-minute bicycle ride from home, are tended by the elderly while the wage earners fish or work elsewhere.

Working at home, a fisherman's wife weaves cloth. Ine women may spend up to 10 hours a day at their looms and may earn more money from their cloth than their men do fishing.

To satisfy fishermen's thirst, Tomio Mukai and son Yoshinaga make and sell their own brand of sake, called Bamboo Dew. The business has been in the family for more than 250 years.

71

To the beat of a cloth-covered drum, Ine men compete in a boat race, part of a festival held on a nearby island that is off limits to women. The entire island

is a Shinto shrine dedicated to the god of wealth and commerce.

Japanese officers survey the damage
done to the Tsar's fleet at Port Arthur,
a Russian outpost in northern China.
During the 1904-1905 Russo-Japanese
War, Japan seized 59 forts around the
city, four battleships and more than 50
other vessels belonging to the foe.

PEOPLE OF THE "DIVINE WIND"

Shortly after dawn on May 27, 1905, a Japanese Navy cruiser emerged from the morning mist near the Tsushima islands in the Korea Strait, the passage between Japan and the Korean peninsula. The cruiser's captain, standing on the bridge, saw before him a daunting sight — a Russian fleet of about 50 warships, steaming northward. Japan's Navy had already outfought and outsmarted most of Russia's Far Eastern naval squadron. This fleet was a new and formidable menace.

The captain ordered full speed and, heeling hard, his cruiser sped away before any Russian guns could be brought to bear. Soon his vessel's wireless operator was sending coded messages through the mist, informing the commander of Japan's battle fleet, Admiral Heihachiro Togo, exactly where the Russian intruders were. The tough, decisive Togo swiftly made his plans. The result would be the first major naval engagement of the 20th Century — and, as history would show, one of the most decisive.

Russia and Japan had been at war for more than a year. At issue were Korea and Manchuria, the one a weak, newly independent country, the other a province of the tottering Chinese Empire. Both Russia and Japan considered them ripe for plucking. The Russians had sent troops into Manchuria and were threatening Korea. Its diplomatic protests having failed, Japan went to war. To the amazement of the world,

tiny Japan's Army as well as its Navy had swiftly taken the measure of its huge opponent's Far Eastern forces, winning decisive battles at the strategic Manchurian naval base of Port Arthur and inland at Mukden.

Russia's only hope of retrieving the situation in the Far East lay with the 50 warships steaming up the Korea Strait. This was the Tsar's Baltic fleet; most of its ships had made an excruciatingly difficult 18,000-mile voyage around Africa, across the Indian Ocean and up the China Sea to challenge Togo's force. The Tsar's orders, given to the commander of the fleet, Admiral Zinovi Petrovich Rozhdestvenski, were concise: "Wipe the infidels off the face of the earth."

The infidels, however, had other plans. Admiral Togo correctly guessed that Rozhdestvenski's immediate goal after so long a voyage was to reach the friendly Siberian port of Vladivostok, there to refit and refuel. Togo's aim was to stop the Russian before he could do so, risking all on an immediate attack despite the fact that Rozhdestvenski had more ships and heavier guns. While his light cruisers shadowed the Russians, Togo led his small battle fleet — four brand-new ironclad battleships and eight heavy cruisers — out of its anchorage in Chinhae Bay on the Korean coast.

Rozhdestvenski also had four modern battleships, including his flagship, *Suvoroff,* and they headed the Russian

3

column. Many of the other Russian vessels, however, were of earlier vintage. Some were heavily armed and armored but so slow that they forced the entire line to steam ahead at a mere nine knots. Togo decided to take advantage of this through speed and deception.

As the Russian fleet proceeded past Tsushima, the Japanese admiral formed up his battle line on the horizon to the northeast. Rozhdestvenski ordered his gunners to meet an attack on the fleet's starboard side. But Togo sent his battleships and cruisers streaking past the head of the Russian column, to wheel and rake the enemy with gunfire from the port side.

The Russian gunners blasted away at the oncoming Japanese vessels but scored few hits. Japanese gunnery was excellent, and shortly Togo's line of battle, which was now reinforced by virtually every ship under his command, was pounding the enemy fleet.

Then Togo once again led his fleet across the head of the Russian column, executing the classic naval maneuver called crossing the T. The massed broadsides of the Japanese formation devastated the flagship *Suvoroff*, destroying her communications gear and seriously wounding Admiral Rozhdestvenski. Now leaderless, the Russian fleet floundered along, unable to make countermaneuvers. Soon thereafter, another large Russian ironclad, the *Oslyabya*, was pulverized and sank, bow forward. A third Russian battleship, *Alexander III*, also took a pounding, eventually to sink along with her sister ship *Borodino*.

As night fell, Japanese destroyers and torpedo boats dashed through the disorganized Russian fleet, sending more wounded enemy warships to the bottom. The next morning most of the remaining Russian vessels, surrounded by Togo's virtually undamaged flotilla, ran up the white flag. Only three of the Tsar's precious ships escaped being sunk or interned.

Japan's victory in the Battle of Tsushima resoundingly ended the Russo-Japanese War. The subsequent peace treaty gave the victors most of what they had fought for, including control of Korea and a foothold in Manchuria.

Togo's triumph also dazzled the world. Everyone knew that the Japanese had been modernizing their once-backward country and forging up-to-date armed forces. But few dreamed that "gallant little Japan," as U.S. newspapers put it, would be able to so decisively thump the Russian bear.

The feat testified to the immense resourcefulness and adaptability of the nation's people. Forty years before, Japan had been an isolated, semifeudal and technologically backward land. Then, in one of the most astonishing turnarounds in history, the Japanese had bought or borrowed virtually every trapping of modernity the Western world had to offer.

By 1905 the Japanese had developed a school system patterned largely on French and German models, had built steel mills closely resembling those in

Britain's industrial Midlands and possessed a brand-new and extensive railroad network. As for the Army, it had been organized after intense study of the French and German military establishments. And Togo's naval forces had been largely modeled on Britain's mighty Royal Navy.

The abilities that made it possible for the Japanese to achieve this sudden self-modernization can be traced far back in Japan's long history. The Japanese exalted hard toil many centuries before the modern factory existed. They had learned how to take the best from an alien culture before the nations of the West had evolved.

Moreover, they were adept warriors long before rifles or battleships had been invented. Japan's history is marked by episodes of fierce internecine struggle between bloodthirsty factions led by outsize warrior heroes. Though they were skilled in the arts of peace, the Japanese could also be intensely bellicose — as would be demonstrated in the Russo-Japanese and Second World Wars.

Most important of all, the Japanese were able to shift virtually overnight from feudalism to modernity because they had for centuries considered themselves a unique and unified people devoted above all to the welfare of their nation. Convinced that modernization was necessary in the 1860s, they "turned on a cultural dime," as one commentator has put it, and threw themselves into the task with remarkable unity of purpose.

This sense of themselves as a unique people derives in part from the fact that the Japanese islands have been dominated by the same ethnic group, with virtually no admixture from outside, for nearly 1,500 years. Most other na-

Terra-cotta figures like this armored warrior dating from the Fifth Century A.D. were placed around earthen tombs perhaps to prevent the soil from slipping and to fend off evil spirits. Such figures are called *haniwa*, which means "cylinder of clay."

tions have taken in immigrants or suffered invasions through the centuries. Not Japan. Never successfully invaded — at least not until the Occupation of 1945 — Japan has never welcomed immigrants either. The population of today's Japan is descended almost exclusively from people who had arrived in the islands by 500 A.D.

The ancestors of the modern Japanese began voyaging to the islands from the Asian mainland before the time of Christ. Most of these settlers appear to have been simple tribespeople who knew how to weave cloth, smelt iron and grow rice in flooded fields. But in the Third or Fourth Century A.D. this peaceful people of the rice paddies evolved into a more warlike group. The warriors divided into clans, or *uji*, and they became the hereditary elite of a strongly aristocratic society.

One clan was soon regarded as preeminent. This was the *uji* that ruled the fertile Yamato plain of Honshu, Japan's main island, and claimed descent from the sun-goddess; they made her the highest of the nature gods, whose collective worship the Japanese came to call Shinto. Soon this dominant clan had elevated their leader to the role of hereditary high priest of the realm — and later to emperor.

It was not long, however, before other clans began usurping the power of the Yamato priest-emperor. Among the first of these upstarts were the Soga, who became supreme at the Yamato court through intermarriage with the imperial clan. Being ambitious, the Soga clansmen soon tried to extend the court's sway into the hinterlands of Honshu, to gather increased tax revenues for themselves and the emperors they dominated.

Dwarfing his brothers in this posthumous Seventh Century painting, Prince Shotoku displays the benign expression of a religious, as well as a secular, leader. One of the first Buddhists in Japan, he encouraged the construction of temples and monasteries.

Standing in their way were other powerful *uji*, jealous of the Soga's power. These rival clansmen were conservative guardians of the Shinto faith. The Soga hit on the bold plan of importing Buddhism from China and Korea; by undermining Shinto they evidently hoped to sap the power of their rivals. This ploy so appalled the more conservative *uji* that they initiated a civil war, from which the Soga emerged victorious in the year 587. The Soga proceeded to expand their pro-Buddhist stance into a huge effort to turn Japan into an island replica of imperial China.

They found an enthusiastic ally in the Empress's nephew, Crown Prince Shotoku, a learned young man who was already a supporter of Buddhism. In 604 Shotoku promulgated a 17-point constitution, based on Chinese models, that introduced the clan nobility to the radical doctrine that Japan's Emperor, like China's, was the country's sole governing power. Three years later the Prince dispatched an official embassy to China with instructions to study the entire range of Chinese culture.

During the next two centuries — and especially after the founding of a capital at Nara in 710 — Japan became a facsimile of the Chinese state, with a

A CHRONOLOGY OF KEY EVENTS

660 B.C. The mythical first Japanese Emperor, Jimmu, regarded as a descendant of the sun-goddess Amaterasu, begins his rule.

57 A.D. Chinese records indicate the arrival of the first Japanese envoy at the Han court, near modern Xian.

c. 405 The Chinese method of writing in characters is imported.

552 Buddhism is officially introduced into Japan.

587 Victory of the pro-Buddhist Soga faction within Japan's ruling Yamato court leads to a more rapid acceptance of Chinese ideas.

607 Prince Shotoku sends emissaries to China to learn more about Chinese institutions, art and culture.

645 Following a coup at the imperial court, a series of reforms, called the Taika Reforms, leads to the creation of a small replica of the Chinese Empire.

710 The construction of the first permanent capital at Nara is completed. The Nara period marks the height of Sinicization efforts.

c. 712 Japan's first history, the *Kojiki (Record of Ancient Matters)*, is written. The second, the *Nihon Shoki (Chronicles of Japan)*, is compiled in 720.

794 A new capital (called Heian, later Kyoto) is built, beginning the Heian period. Under the Fujiwara family, art and culture flourish.

838 The last of the great Japanese missions leaves for China's T'ang court.

900-1000 A new system of phonetic writing called *kana* develops, allowing prose works to flourish.

c. 1010 Japanese prose attains new sophistication with *The Tale of Genji*, a work by Lady Murasaki *(below)*.

1156 A dispute over the imperial succession brings rival warrior clans into open conflict in Kyoto. The court and the city suffer heavily before Kiyomori, leader of the Taira clan, emerges triumphant in 1160.

1185 The Kamakura period begins as the Minamoto clan crushes the Taira family after five years of struggle. Yoritomo *(below)* takes the title of shogun

in 1192 and rules from Kamakura, near today's Tokyo. This begins the early feudal period.

1191 Zen Buddhism (Rinzai sect) is introduced from China.

1274 Mongols make their first attempt to invade Japan.

1281 Destruction of the Mongol fleet by a typhoon ends the second Mongol invasion attempt.

1331 Emperor Godaigo rebels against the Kamakura shoguns. Rival courts exist at Kyoto and Nara until 1392.

1338 The Ashikaga shogunate is set up in Kyoto; its power erodes as feudal lords reassert themselves. The political chaos lasts through the 15th Century.

1384 Kanami, creator of *noh* drama, in which actors wear masks *(below)*, dies.

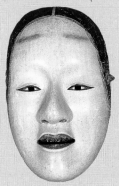

1542 or 1543 Portuguese merchants and navigators, the first Westerners to set foot in Japan, arrive in Tanegashima, an island off the southern coast of Kyushu. They introduce Western firearms.

1549 St. Francis Xavier becomes the first Christian missionary to journey to Japan.

1568 Oda Nobunaga, a minor but ambitious feudal lord — and a master of military strategy — seizes Kyoto and begins reunifying the country.

1582 Toyotomi Hideyoshi, son of a common soldier, assumes power when Nobunaga is assassinated.

1597-1598 Hideyoshi expels Christian missionaries and commences a second campaign against Korea. The effort is abandoned not long after his death in 1598.

1600 Tokugawa clan leader Ieyasu *(below)* defeats a coalition of rivals and

succeeds Hideyoshi. Ieyasu initiates the rigid, isolationist political system that characterizes the two and a half centuries of the Tokugawa shogunate.

1603 The first performances of *kabuki*, Japan's popular drama, take place in a Kyoto theater.

1636 Japanese are forbidden to travel outside Japan by Ieyasu's grandson, Iemitsu.

1639 Europeans residing in Japan are expelled in the wake of a Christian rebellion near Nagasaki. Only the Dutch are allowed to stay, living in virtual imprisonment on the island of Deshima, in Nagasaki harbor.

1657 Edo burns.

1688-1704 During this era, known as Genroku, Japanese popular culture flourishes in the cities, among the growing merchant class.

1853 American warships under the command of Commodore Matthew C. Perry arrive in Edo Bay *(below)*. Trea-

ties with the U.S., Great Britain, Russia and the Netherlands follow.

1868 The Tokugawa shogunate is overthrown; the Meiji period begins as the new imperial government is established in Tokyo.

1871 Old class distinctions begin to be abolished. Compulsory elementary education is instituted in 1872.

1877 The government quells the last revolt of the old privileged warrior (samurai) class.

1889 Japan's first constitution provides for a bicameral legislature, the Diet.

1894-1895 As a result of the Sino-Japanese War *(below)*, Japan gains control of Taiwan, the Pescadores, Port Arthur and the Liaotung peninsula.

1905 Victory in the Russo-Japanese War (1904-1905) raises Japan to the status of a world power.

1910 Japan officially annexes Korea.

1914 Japan joins the Allied side in World War I.

1923 The great Tokyo earthquake kills more than 130,000.

1931 The military takeover of Manchuria leads to the creation in 1932 of the puppet state of Manchukuo.

1933 Japan pulls out of the League of Nations because of an international protest over the seizure of Manchuria.

1937 The Japanese invasion of China alienates the U.S., Britain and other Western democracies. The drift toward World War II accelerates as Japan signs a tripartite alliance with Fascist Germany and Italy in 1940.

1941 Japan launches a surprise air attack on Pearl Harbor. Japanese forces press their conquest of Southeast Asia.

1942-1943 The naval battles of the Coral Sea and Midway partially cripple the Japanese Navy and reverse the course of the war in the Pacific. U.S. and Australian ground and air forces begin the "island-hopping" campaigns that will help defeat Japan.

1945 Atomic bombs are dropped on Hiroshima and Nagasaki; Japan surrenders, and World War II ends. The democratization process begins under the Allied Occupation.

1947 A new democratic constitution goes into effect, stripping the Emper-

or of all power and extending the franchise to men and women over 20.

1952 The Occupation ends.

1956 Japan enters the United Nations.

1960 The renewal of the Japan-U.S. Mutual Security Treaty sparks widespread demonstrations *(below)*.

1960-1970 Japan's gross national product grows at an average annual rate of 10.4 per cent.

1964 The bullet train starts its run between Tokyo and Osaka. Construction begins on the 33-mile-long Seikan Undersea Tunnel, linking the islands of Honshu and Hokkaido.

1968-1969 Fifty Japanese universities, including Tokyo University, virtually cease to function as the result of a decade of student unrest that culminates in riots. Some 20,000 people are arrested before peace returns to the nation's campuses.

1972 Japan resumes diplomatic and trade relations with China.

1973-1974 The Arab oil embargo jolts the Japanese economy. As a consequence, Japan experiences its first postwar decline in industrial production, along with severe inflation.

1985 Premier Yasuhiro Nakasone, in an effort to prevent an international trade war, appeals to his countrymen to buy more foreign goods.

central government and an increasingly cultured court. The more docile clansmen gave up their armor to wear long Chinese-style robes. Palaces were modeled after Chinese examples. Government records were inscribed in Chinese characters. Buddhism flourished — and would from then on have an influence on Japanese manners and ways of thinking.

The Chinese idea that the Emperor was the source of all authority also caught hold. Japan's Emperor through the subsequent centuries has seldom wielded any real political power, but the nation's actual rulers — nobles or feudal lords, generals or prime ministers — have always governed in the Emperor's name, his remote and godlike presence giving their regimes legitimacy and helping to unite the people behind them. As a result, the imperial family has been inviolate, surviving all the violent twists and turns of Japan's history. The Emperors of the 20th Century are direct descendants of those who emerged on the Yamato plain more than a millennium and a half ago.

The wholesale importation of Chinese ways begun by Shotoku revealed a fundamental Japanese trait — a genius for borrowing from other cultures. The Soga, who had largely inspired the process, fell victims of a palace coup in the year 645. Their successors as wielders of the power behind the imperial throne were members of an even more ambitious and successful clan, the Fujiwara. By marrying their daughters into the imperial family, the Fujiwara eventually gained control of the court and the government, and they proceeded to run the country for about 500 years.

The hothouse atmosphere of the Fujiwara-dominated court, much like that of some of the self-absorbed princely courts of Renaissance Europe, produced beautiful and exotic blooms. Especially after the Emperor moved his capital in 794 from Nara to Heian — later known as Kyoto — literature and other arts flourished as never before. But like many other refined courts, this one invited its own destruction. The Chinese-style central government became feeble, in part because the Fujiwara and other nobles — along with numerous Buddhist monasteries and Shinto shrines — had wangled tax-free status for their vast landholdings. With tax revenues thus substantially reduced, the government and its ministries inevitably decayed.

Into the vacuum rushed restless and power-hungry men from the hinterlands. Some had begun as estate managers for the nobles who were living a languorous life at court. In the absence of attention from the decayed government ministries, these de facto rulers of the rural regions settled local disputes and collected rents for their absentee landlords. Attached to the great estates were hardy warriors called *bushi* (later, samurai) who protected the countryside from roving brigands. The fierce *bushi* recognized no allegiance higher than personal loyalty to their own military chiefs. They ignored the authority of the nobles at court.

The eclipse of the Fujiwara government began in 1156 when two court factions became embroiled in a contest over which member of the imperial family should become the next Emperor. One faction imprudently asked the Minamoto, the largest landholders in eastern Honshu, to support its cause. The rival faction then sought support from the Taira clansmen from western Honshu. When the two clans and their warrior bands met head on in Kyoto, that elegant sanctuary of the court nobility became the scene of destruction and cruelty.

Warriors burst into the city's palaces, slaying the cowering courtiers within. Bowmen shot court ladies as they fled from buildings that had been put to the torch. "Those who were afraid of the arrows and terrified by the flames," a chronicler of the time reported, "even jumped into wells in large numbers, and of these, too, the bottom ones in a short time had drowned, those in the middle were crushed to death by their fellows."

When the slaughter was over, the Taira had routed the Minamoto. The most powerful man in Japan, in control of both Emperor and court, was now the Taira leader, Kiyomori. But Kiyomori made what would prove a fatal mistake. Instead of founding a vigorous new regime, he joined the old one, aping the manners of the surviving court aristocracy and, in time-honored fashion, wedding his daughter to a member of the imperial family.

Kiyomori's failure to create a new government alienated the warriors who had brought him to power. This gave the Minamoto their chance. Rallying the disgruntled warriors, the Minamoto leader, Yoritomo, led a revolt against the Taira-dominated court. In a bitter five-year war, he seized control of central Honshu, forced the Taira from Kyoto and finally defeated them in a naval battle on the Inland Sea.

Learning from Kiyomori's mistakes, Yoritomo remained brazenly independent of the court and its effete nobility. To underscore that independence, he set up a separate government not in Kyoto, but in the seaside village of Kamakura, today a Tokyo suburb. The

More than 700 years old, this precious scroll from the Imperial Household Collection records a high point in the battle between the Japanese and the Mongols in 1281. Here, Japanese warriors board an enemy ship to kill the Mongol leader.

sort of government he founded would rule Japan for the next 700 years.

This government has come to be called the shogunate because Yoritomo and his successors bore the title of shogun, "the Emperor's general." The Emperor, as before and since, was theoretically the nation's ruler — and indeed continued to preside in Kyoto over a much reduced and often impoverished court. But Yoritomo and the shoguns who immediately followed him did the actual ruling, maintaining their power base in Kamakura, which gave its name to the first era of shogunate rule.

During the early Kamakura period the shoguns appointed constables drawn from the warrior class to administer Japan's provinces. Under the constables were stewards who administered the great estates. They in turn were served by bands of other warriors. The government was, in short, a sort of military dictatorship with the power to rule every aspect of Japanese life. It could be cruelly arbitrary, but it also helped give the Japanese people a sense of belonging to a single homogeneous

nation centuries before Britain, France, Germany or Italy were anything but fractious clusters of dukedoms and principalities.

The shogunate endured many changes over the succeeding centuries. The shogun himself at times became, like the Emperor, a figurehead, with the real decision-making power in the hands of a committee of shadowy counselors. This, too, would leave an indelible imprint on Japanese life: Collective and anonymous decision making has remained a favored Japanese strategy in commerce and politics.

Yoritomo, however, stayed firmly and solely in charge until his death in 1199, and the Kamakura regime retained the vigor of youth long after that. Within the next century the once-humble fighting men of the hinterlands, elevated to positions of power by Yoritomo, repaid their countrymen in full measure as Japan faced the greatest crises in its history.

Black clouds first loomed in 1268 when Kublai Khan, grandson of the all-conquering Genghis, sent an emissary

to Japan demanding submission to his rule. As the Japanese well knew, the Mongol war machine's swift-wheeling cavalry, with a contingent of Korean infantry, had already conquered an immense empire stretching from Korea to the Adriatic. All the defenders had were their swords and a grim code of honor, *bushido,* which demanded unswerving loyalty to one's sworn leader and an utter disregard of death.

In November of 1274, twenty-five thousand Mongol-led troops landed on the northern coast of Kyushu. The Japanese warriors, uncowed by the Mongol weapons and numbers, fell upon the invaders and fought them to a standstill in a furious, day-long engagement. When the Korean seamen who had brought the Mongol invaders warned that a storm was brewing, the Mongols gladly withdrew to their ships.

This setback did not end the threat. Ruling their empire through fear, the Mongols could ill afford to tolerate a defiantly independent Japan. Again the Great Khan sent ambassadors to the islands, ordering "the King of Japan" to

3

pay him homage at Peking. The Kamakura officials replied in the most contemptuous way they knew; they cut off the envoys' heads. Then, in an amazing display of national unity, a great army gathered to meet the Mongol reprisal.

The second Mongol invasion began in early June of 1281 as two fleets carrying a total of 150,000 men converged on western Japan. Once again they failed to terrify the Japanese defenders. The fighting went on for 50 days before a typhoon swept over Kyushu, wrecking the Mongol ships. The hard-pressed invaders were demoralized by the loss of their only means of retreat. Some fell to Japanese swords; many others surrendered. The Japanese called this unforgettably timely storm "the divine wind," or *kamikaze,* and cherished it as proof that the gods protected Japan from invaders.

The great victory of 1281 added to the glory of the warrior class. At the same time, it had the ironic effect of undermining the government Yoritomo had founded. The warriors had given their all to the regime, but it had run out of lands or offices to give in return. In 1331, angry swordsmen, coming to the aid of a disgruntled Emperor, revolted against the Kamakura government and brought it down.

What replaced it was not a new form of rule — or even the old imperial system — but merely a weaker shogunate, followed in the mid-15th Century by sheer anarchy. "The age of the overthrow of the higher by the lower," the Japanese called it, as lesser warrior leaders overthrew great lords, and Buddhist congregations of peasants and townsmen, infected by the prevailing violence, rose in furious revolts.

This century of lawless energy transformed Japan into a fragmented society resembling that of feudal Europe. The country found itself divided into hundreds of independent domains, each ruled by a lord called a daimyo. The feudal rulers lived in moated castles and supported bands of retainers, now called samurai, loyal vassals, who held fiefs of land in return for providing armed protection.

Some of the prouder and more intelligent feudal lords were repelled by their country's condition. A young but ambitious daimyo, the 17-year-old Oda Nobunaga — who would become one of the most ruthless leaders in Japanese history — took the first unwitting step toward reunification in 1551. Struggling to retain his newly inherited position as family head against armed bands led by his own jealous kinsmen, Nobunaga raised a force of about 1,000 men and soundly defeated his rivals.

Gaining confidence in his own military abilities, Nobunaga gathered larger armies and took the field against more potent enemies. By 1559 he was the master of Owari province, near the present-day city of Nagoya. The next year he surprised a hostile force of 25,000 men in a narrow ravine and thrashed them — although his own army numbered only 4,000. This victory brought Nobunaga fame and a host of new allies. By the late 1560s he was so powerful that he succeeded in taking over the old capital of Kyoto.

Still, enemies roamed the hinterlands. Nobunaga sallied forth to meet them. In his rampages through Honshu, he showed mercy to no one. When a faithful uncle, successful in battle, became too popular among the members of the clan, Nobunaga had him murdered. When a Buddhist monastery on Mount Hiei openly allied itself with his enemies, Nobunaga stunned all Japan by burning down its 3,000 buildings and slaughtering every man, woman and child caught fleeing from the flames. By the time an assassin cut down the conqueror in 1582, Nobunaga had made himself master of most of central Japan.

The task of completing the country's unification fell to Nobunaga's great assistant general, Toyotomi Hideyoshi. Returning from campaigns in western Honshu to avenge Nobunaga's death, Hideyoshi seized control of central Japan. By 1590 he had brought the remainder of the recalcitrant daimyo to heel and placed the nation under one central authority.

Hideyoshi would go to any lengths to

In a rare depiction of Christian rites in early 17th Century Japan, a priest and followers worship at an altar. There were more than 300,000 Christian converts in the country at the time.

keep the country unified, and that was in some respects unfortunate. A new Japan seemed to be developing. Once-rigid class lines had blurred during the years of anarchy. Peasants had become warriors, and samurai had taken to the sea, carrying on a thriving commerce throughout Southeast Asia. The Japanese were importing all manner of new ideas from abroad.

Hideyoshi did much to halt this promising ferment. His successor, a member of the Tokugawa clan named Ieyasu, also tried to stamp out new and alien ideas. The insulating process was completed by Ieyasu's successors, his son and grandson. In the name of national unity, these conservative shoguns slammed shut Japan's doors. During the entire 268-year Tokugawa period, the nation was cut off from virtually every outside influence. All foreigners were expelled from the country, including dozens of Christian missionaries. In 1636 an edict forbade all Japanese from leaving the country; any attempt to do so was punishable by death. The only peephole to the outside world was an island in the harbor of Nagasaki visited annually by a Dutch ship and by a few Chinese traders.

The Tokugawa shogunate forced Japan back into a rigid feudalism. The daimyo continued as lords of their domains, and the samurai became a hereditary elite that filled most official positions. The peasants were enmeshed in endless restrictions. They were forbidden to leave the land, to ride horses, to carry swords or to use family names (the use of a surname was a symbol of aristocratic status). Authorities prescribed the peasants' clothes and hairdos and decreed a thousand petty rules

A lifesaving device, this fan was carried into battle by a samurai who used its iron end plates to parry the blows of his enemy's sword or spear. The gold-inlaid end plates bear images of animals of the zodiac.

A captioned diagram indicates the cuts a samurai can make on a beheaded criminal's corpse to improve his swordplay. The cuts varied in difficulty, from a simple slash across the hips to the lopping off of a hand with one quick and well-aimed blow.

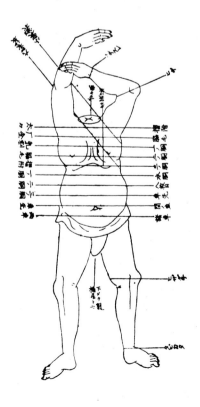

of etiquette. These the samurai could enforce with a severe beating or even with the deadly slash of their swords.

The self-discipline and obedience that have long characterized the Japanese were strengthened during the harsh years of Tokugawa rule.

In the Tokugawa class system, craftsmen ranked even lower than peasants, and merchants lowest of all. Yet nobody thrived more than the merchants during the centuries of Tokugawa peace. This unintended outcome was largely the result of the government's obsession with stability. In order to control the feudal lords, the Tokugawa rulers compelled them to leave their wives and heirs as hostages in Edo — today's Tokyo — the town where Ieyasu had set up his government. One year out of every two, the daimyo themselves had to be present in Edo. Under this hostage system, Edo became a place where the daimyo and their retinues vied with one another in conspicuous consumption. By 1700 the new capital had a population of more than half a million. Meanwhile, the samurai, who were now paid cash stipends by their daimyo, became a nationwide consumer class numbering two million.

Many merchant families, taking advantage of this new consumerism, assembled huge fortunes during the Tokugawa period. One commercial dynasty was founded by an unemployed samurai who was a member of the Mitsui family. On a visit to Edo, he was struck by the number of people living there. Returning home, he announced that he intended to exchange the empty honor of samurai status for the lowly but challenging life of a merchant. "I have seen that great profits can be

83

3

made honorably," he told his kinsmen. "I shall brew sake and soy sauce and we shall prosper."

The Mitsui did indeed start modestly with a sake shop in their native village of Matsusaka. After years of scrimping, the eldest son was sent into Edo, where he opened the draper's shop that would be the foundation of the family's commercial empire. The Mitsui saw clearly that a money economy was rapidly replacing the old rural barter system. In time they set up a large new retail shop in Edo run on a decidedly modern basis: modest goods, fixed prices, cash only. When the Tokugawa regime collapsed in 1868, Mitsui was one of the few great merchant houses able to thrive in the revolutionary new world that replaced it.

A sign that the end of the Tokugawa feudal order was not far off came in July 1853, when U.S. Commodore Matthew C. Perry cruised into Edo Bay with two sailing ships, two steam frigates and a pair of demands from President Millard Fillmore. Japan was to provide humane treatment for shipwrecked mariners and must open its ports to American ships. Ominously, Perry warned the Tokugawa leaders that he would return for an answer "with a much larger force."

The shogunate capitulated, agreeing to Perry's original demands. Japan would be open to United States trade. Following a treaty with Russia, Japan would also grant American mariners and merchants the right to be tried in U.S. consular courts under American law rather than Japanese law. When pressed by other Western powers, the Edo regime granted them similar concessions.

The nation's proud daimyo and samurai were angered by these events.

Wearing exaggerated geta, or clogs, to elevate them from the ground, courtesans mince through the main street of Yoshiwara, Tokyo's pleasure district. Yoshiwara has flourished since the early 17th Century.

Two energetic feudal domains in western Japan did something about it. On southern Kyushu the wealthy Satsuma family began building its own navy. In the domain of Choshu in western Honshu, radical young samurai defied the Tokugawa class system and created rifle regiments that mingled samurai and peasants. In 1866 the government in Edo sent an army to Choshu to punish the wayward vassals, but the outnumbered riflemen won the battle.

That was the final blow for the shogunate. On January 3, 1868, rebellious samurai from Choshu and Satsuma, backed by other domains and by key nobles at the imperial court, seized control of Kyoto's imperial palace and the person of the 15-year-old Emperor Mutsuhito. In his name they abolished the shogunate and declared the "restoration" of imperial rule. The next year the new leaders of Japan moved the young Emperor from Kyoto to Edo, duly renamed Tokyo, "the eastern capital." The Emperor's reign was dubbed Meiji, which means "enlightened rule." The great modernization of Japan was about to begin.

Once they understood what was going on, the majority of the Japanese people backed the changes that their new leaders, the "Men of Meiji," were making in the Emperor's name. The national pride had been stung by the "unequal treaties." All wanted Japan to become "the equal of the powers." So cleverly did the young oligarchs spread the idea that they were effecting a "restoration" of the old imperial system that even staunch traditionalists were won over. A number of daimyo voluntarily surrendered their lands to the Emperor even before the leaders decreed that the feudal domains no longer existed. In the early 1870s the Meiji leaders began dismantling the Tokugawa class system, removing all occupational restrictions.

With the heaviest baggage from the past heaved overboard, the Meiji leaders determined to send a great delegation to study the West, just as their ancestors, beginning almost 1,300 years before, had sent emissaries to study China. The embassy set sail from Yokohama in December of 1871 for a grand tour of Western civilization.

Between their arrival in San Francisco in January 1872 and their departure from Europe in the autumn of 1873, the Japanese travelers were treated to a truly eye-opening education. One Meiji leader was both repelled and impressed by Britain's industrial heartland. "Everywhere we go there is nothing growing in the ground, just coal and iron," he wrote in a letter, adding that "factories have increased to an unheard-of extent." He ended by noting that "this is a sufficient explanation of England's wealth and strength." The Chancellor of imperial Germany, Otto von Bismarck, left a deep impression, too. In political matters, authoritarian Germany, rather than liberal England or democratic America, seemed the right model to the men of the Meiji era.

The emissaries returned to their country convinced that if Japan was to become the equal of the Western powers, a vast transformation would have to take place. Exploiting the agricultural wealth of the country, they quickly began laying the foundations of a modern economy: port facilities and lighthouses, a telegraph system, modern central banking, compulsory elementary education, a new legal code. The entire country appeared to be swept up in the Westernizing enterprise. By 1879 children all over Japan were singing the "Civilization Ball Song," accompanying each bounce of a ball with one of the 10 desirable Western things: gas lamps, steam engines, horse-drawn carriages, cameras, telegraphs, lightning rods, newspapers, schools, a letter post and steamboats.

Yet the Meiji leaders did not cherish Western civilization for its own sake. To them, the borrowings were always a means to an end. That end was national strength — the power to revoke the unequal treaties and compel the great nations of the world to accept Japan as one of their number. Enrich the Nation, Strengthen the Army became the national slogan.

The Men of Meiji spurned modern institutions that seemed to threaten national unity. There was little room for democracy, which they feared would be divisive and weakening. When they promulgated a constitution in 1889, they severely limited the powers of the Diet, or parliament, that it established — and only 1 per cent of the population was given the vote. Where traditional beliefs strengthened the government, the Meiji leaders exploited them to the fullest. In order to inspire popular devotion to the state, the oligarchs turned reverence for the Emperor into a pervasive national cult.

Despite the dictatorial rule of the Meiji leaders, forces demanding a more democratic system grew up. A people's-rights movement succeeded in electing a powerful antigovernment bloc to the Diet, in giving the Diet more control over cabinet decisions and eventually in extending the franchise to all males 25 and older. These moderate forces were doomed to defeat by militant nationalists as Japan slid toward war in the 1930s, but they provided lessons in democracy that would be of value later.

A fierce national pride in Japan's growing strength manifested itself even before 1900. So many people felt that the country should make bolder use of its increasingly strong army that the Meiji leaders — normally cautious in foreign affairs — felt compelled to oblige. In 1894 they dispatched troops to drive Chinese forces out of Korea, and 10 years after that they launched a full-scale war against Russia to protect Japan's interests on the Asian mainland, defeating tsarist forces both on land and at sea.

A samurai manages a proud pose in a photograph taken in the 1870s, when the new Meiji government downgraded his class. In early feudal times, prior to engaging in combat, samurai would announce their names, their ancestry and their acts of heroism.

Japan's victory over Russia proved a turning point in the nation's history. In the aftermath of triumph, popular pride in the military grew boundless. So, too, did the military's faith in itself, especially the Army's. Like the old samurai class, the leaders of the new conscript army began to regard themselves as the embodiment of the nation and the guardians of its spirit, what the Japanese called "the national essence."

The shadow of militarism was all the more menacing because, as the original Meiji leaders passed from the scene, their successors tended to be corrupt, routinely accepting bribes from men who wanted their commercial interests advanced. It seemed to many Japanese — among whom poverty was still widespread — that the military men were indeed the only ones who cared for the national essence. When the worldwide economic depression of the late 1920s and early 1930s crippled the Japanese economy, the military struck down the civilian establishment. Nobody rose to defend it.

The first major blow fell on September 18, 1931, when Army conspirators in Manchuria staged a fake sabotage of the Japanese-owned South Manchurian Railroad. Blaming it on Chinese troops, Japanese forces, led by ultra-nationalistic younger officers, immediately overran Manchuria without a shred of official approval. The civilian government stood by helplessly as the entire nation applauded the military's conquest. On that fateful September day, Japan took its first step into "the dark valley," as the Japanese call the lurid, bloodstained decade that preceded World War II.

In the excitement of the hour, ultranationalists began calling for reforms that would purge Japan of its corrupt politicians and greedy capitalists. For some young fanatics, murder was the preferred purgative. In February 1932, while the Army was transforming Manchuria into a puppet state called Manchukuo, assassins cut down the chief director of the huge Mitsui company and the Minister of Finance. Three months later a group of young Navy officers and Army cadets killed 75-year-old Prime Minister Tsuyoshi Inukai for trying to check the military's usurpation of power.

A climax of violence was reached in 1936, when a group of young Army officers attempted to overthrow the government by fanning out through Tokyo at dawn, assassinating every political leader they could locate, including two former Prime Ministers. The coup d'état failed, but the military leaders managed nevertheless to turn the bloody incident to their advantage, in effect warning the nation's civilian politicians that even worse uprisings might occur should the civilians attempt to thwart the Army's will.

In July 1937, a skirmish broke out between Chinese and Japanese troops near Peking, toward which Japan's Manchurian Army had been inching since 1932. Over the objections of the more conservative Navy and the Prime Minister, the Imperial Army launched a full-scale invasion of China. Then in 1940 Japanese troops seized part of French Indochina. With Europe embroiled in a desperate war, the other European colonies of Southeast Asia — rich in rubber, rice and other commodities — seemed easy pickings.

But before Japan moved to scoop up these spoils, the United States, Great Britain and the Netherlands, alarmed by Japanese expansionism, imposed an embargo on the shipment of oil to Japan. Japan's leaders were stunned. Without imported oil the country was doomed to economic strangulation. The government swiftly entered into negotiations with the U.S.

America's demands were uncompromising: complete Japanese withdrawal from China, Manchuria and Indochina. Materially, it was a price Japan could have paid. Withdrawal from the

In one of World War II's most famous pictures, a Chinese baby wounded by a Japanese bomb wails at Shanghai's South Station. During its China campaign, Japan lost 60,000 men and left some two million Chinese dead.

3

Asian mainland would have inflicted only moderate damage on the Japanese economy. The humiliation such a move would have inflicted on the Imperial Army, however, was beyond calculation. Overawed by the terrible, towering pride of the Army, Japan's civilian leaders gave way. In September 1941, the cabinet decided to prepare for war with the United States.

The Japanese leaders did not believe that their country could prevail in a protracted struggle with the most powerful industrial nation in the world. Their plan for victory rested at bottom on a political conviction — that a peace-loving democracy like the U.S. would not have the fortitude to endure a long, bloody war of attrition. It took a savage conflict to teach the Japanese how mistaken their leaders had been.

The Japanese at war demonstrated a baffling mixture of their national strengths and weaknesses. The soldiers of the Army fought with a fanatical devotion to duty, like the samurai of old, often holding out to the last man in the jungles of New Guinea and the Philippines and on such tiny island battlefields as Saipan, Tarawa and Iwo Jima. On many Pacific scenes of battle, U.S. and Australian infantry learned to live in terror of banzai charges — waves of

Japanese troops hurling themselves suicidally at enemy positions.

There was a distinctly vicious side to this fanaticism as well. Because of their abhorrence of surrender, Japanese officers and men looked with contempt on Allied prisoners — and in many instances treated them with abominable cruelty. Almost 27,000 of the 95,000 British, American and other prisoners in Japanese hands died during the

Aboard the U.S. battleship *Missouri*, anchored in Tokyo Bay, the Japanese delegation stands ready to sign the document formalizing their country's surrender. Earlier, the Emperor had told his military to "bear the unbearable" and accept defeat.

War, of disease, malnutrition, overwork and physical abuse. And many of the civilian inhabitants of Burma, Thailand, Malaya and the other countries the Japanese conquered so swiftly in 1942 perished performing what amounted to slave labor.

As the onetime conquerors were inexorably pushed back toward the Japanese home islands, the inhabitants of those islands began to pay a dreadful price for their leaders' arrogance. Depleted food stocks brought privation and, with it, rampant diseases. Then came the bombs. In one raid alone, that of March 10, 1945, B-29s loosed 2,000 tons of incendiaries over Tokyo, immolating 100,000 people in one night. Months of fire raids followed. And on August 6 and 9 came the most fearful destruction of all, the two atomic blasts that leveled the cities of Hiroshima and Nagasaki. The horror ended at noon on August 15, 1945, when over their radios the Japanese people heard a high-pitched voice only a very few of them had ever heard before. It was the Emperor himself, announcing that Japan had indeed lost the War.

When Allied Occupation forces arrived in Japan — the first alien troops ever to set foot on Japanese soil in victory — they found the people, in the words of one writer, "dazed, tottering, numb with shock." Observed their new Supreme Commander, U.S. General Douglas MacArthur: "It was not merely the overthrow of their military might — it was the collapse of a faith, it was the disintegration of everything they believed in and lived by and fought for."

The ancient virtues of the Japanese people, however, had not disintegrated. The discipline that made them so formidable in war still served them in

the hour of catastrophe. Their capacity for work overcame their exhaustion. Their aptitude for cooperative endeavor overcame anarchy. Schooled in the arts of frugality, they began repairing their devastated land with every usable scrap that could be scrounged from the wreckage.

Shattered though they were by defeat, the Japanese blamed not the enemy but their own leaders and the militaristic fervor that dated back to the 1930s — and in which most of them had shared. As they pulled themselves together, they began reaching for some new and better way.

In the first months of the Occupation, a newly popular word was heard everywhere: *demokurashi*. Many Japanese had only a limited notion of what it meant. That it was powerful was obvious enough. It was also benevolent. Its towering incarnation, the Supreme Commander, performed astonishing feats, extending suffrage to the women of Japan and forcing the country's 160,000 absentee landlords to sell their farms to their tenant farmers. *Demokurashi* treated the Japanese people with greater respect than many of them felt for themselves.

Democracy could be extremely disturbing — reducing the Emperor to a symbol stripped of all power and divinity, and extending to workers the right to form unions and bargain collectively. But it clearly held out a great hope to a proud and patriotic people. On April 10, 1946, an impressive majority of the adult population went to the polls and voted overwhelmingly for candidates who supported the country's first bona fide democratic constitution. The Japanese had again joined together to help their nation through another momentous change. □

Simplicity itself, this room in a modern yet traditional Japanese house was built according to a standard unit of measure based on the dimensions of a straw mat, or tatami. Even doors and windows correspond to the tatami's size.

ART AS A WAY OF LIFE

The 800-year-old juniper, its bleached trunk split by some long-ago catastrophe, twists from the earth in two tortured segments. Above the scarred wood, the tree's needles form spiky cushions of green that cast deep shadows on the mossy ground.

The weathered tree could be growing along a deserted seacoast or windswept mountainside. Instead, it stands in a shallow tray, its roots clinging to a thin layer of soil. This tiny tree — no more than two feet tall — has been in the care of a single family for generations. Saburo Kato, its present keeper, is the son and grandson of *bonsai* masters, professional growers of miniature trees that have been trained into graceful shapes by years of pruning and wiring of branches.

The art of *bonsai* is an ancient one, and Kato is among its foremost living practitioners. But unlike other artists, a *bonsai* master can never complete a project. Kato will patiently, gently, shape a tree through a lifetime of seasons — and when he dies, another master will pick up where he left off.

Small, restrained, evocative — in all these characteristics a *bonsai* reflects the Japanese sense of beauty, an esthetic that prizes the fragility and the uncertainty of life itself. And in providing a living connection with the past, a *bonsai* also epitomizes the Japanese reverence for tradition.

Bound to a mountainous land where living space is scarce, the Japanese have put a premium on the inner space of the mind. In their art and culture, they have chosen, perhaps inevitably, to emphasize restraint and contemplation. The sweeping epics of Homer or Dante, the vast, colorful canvases of Titian or Raphael are the antithesis of the Japanese esthetic.

For the Japanese, nuance is all. Kato's 800-year-old *bonsai* is nature distilled, concentrated, the embodiment, as well as the ideal, of the essential tree. Similarly, the country's most popular form of poetry, the 17-syllable *haiku*, is a marvel of compressed expression. The traditional forms of Japanese drama — *noh, kabuki, bunraku* — are performed with highly stylized movements, distilled hundreds of years ago from a range of gestures. And ancient Japanese *sumi-e*, or ink painting, captures subjects from nature in a few deft strokes of brush and ink, leaving the viewer to mentally fill in the missing elements.

To an extent that continually astounds visitors, the Japanese incorporate their esthetic into everyday life. While employing all the technical marvels of the modern age to advance themselves, they preserve and cherish their past. This ability to balance the old and the new derives from their ancient religion, Shinto, which emphasizes the natural order of things and encourages the acceptance of that order.

Thus, although the Japanese live in unprepossessing, urban surroundings, they make room for beauty in innumerable small ways. Every spring, the ephemeral blossoming of the cherry trees attracts millions of Japanese to choice viewing sites all over the country. And almost everyone, it seems, can — and does — write poetry. At least a million new *haiku* are printed each year, in dozens of magazines devoted to the art.

Similarly, few homes are without a *tokonoma*, an alcove in which a scroll may be hung or a tasteful display of flowers set out according to rules prescribed in *ikebana*, the classical art of flower arranging. Schools that teach *ikebana* are extremely popular, as are similar schools devoted to the teaching of *cha-no-yu* — the contemplative art of the tea ceremony.

Although quietness and rigorous control are the characteristics most often associated with Japanese art, they coexist with a contrasting mood. Where the *noh* drama is one of severe formalism, *kabuki* is loud, boisterous and filled with color. And whereas *sumi-e* is a model of understatement, with its brushwork in black and shades of gray, many classic wood-block prints are almost comic-book caricatures of brazen courtesans or *kabuki* actors rendered in bright colors.

These contradictory traits can be at least partially explained by the fact that many elements of Japanese art and culture were originally imported from China, starting in about 300 A.D. and ending in the 16th Century. But the Japanese never, as one authority stated it, "surrendered the inmost stronghold of their own tradition." They could accept the simplicity of Buddhism because their own Shintoism already valued it, and their practicality enabled them to counterbalance the Chinese in-

fluence with strengths of their own. Thus in *noh* performances, the somber dramatic style influenced by imported Zen Buddhism is relieved by comic interludes in colloquial language. Everything Japan took from China was, in the words of another expert, "filtered through the basically different Japanese temperament" — a process continuing today in the face of Western influences.

More than 1,000 years ago, Japan

borrowed China's ideographic script, called *kanji* in Japanese. From it evolved two sets of phonetic symbols, jointly called *kana*. All three systems are used concurrently today, but a thousand years ago they were not. *Kanji*, the Chinese script, was the system used by scholars, priests and officials, and was the primary province of men. Women, for the most part, did not use *kanji*, but wrote *kana*, the phonetic script.

More than 100 years old, a miniature red maple reflects the patient training of several generations of *bonsai* masters. Such a tree, if it were for sale, might fetch as much as $10,000.

Rather than being handicapped, however, women were thus enabled to record spoken Japanese in a way that was impossible for men who could use only *kanji*. Consequently, for a period of about 100 years, almost every noteworthy author who wrote in Japanese was a woman — a rare and perhaps unique phenomenon in the world's cultural history.

The most extraordinary work to be produced during that period was written by a member of the Heian imperial court, Lady Murasaki. About Lady Murasaki herself very little is known, but her descriptions of court life reveal a discerning eye, and her book, *The Tale of Genji*, begun in about 1000 A.D. and finished some 20 years later, has been called the world's first novel.

The story of a "shining prince" who, while carrying on a succession of love affairs, becomes the most powerful statesman of the realm, *The Tale of Genji* depicts the esthetic sensibility and the pervasiveness of poetry in the life of the aristocracy. No important event was complete without the writing and exchanging of commemorative poems, and *Genji* contains some 800 original verses, ascribed to the many characters in the novel.

At court, entire conversations between lovers were carried on in poems. A felicitous verse might win a woman's favors — or send an unwanted suitor packing. How the poem was dispatched was also significant, and an ardent writer would attach a spray of flowers to his or her note. Failure to compose an appropriate poem on some auspicious occasion such as the first snowfall of the year could be considered a serious social blunder. Finally, the poem had to be presented in an elegant hand, for calligraphy was already a sister art to poetry, and many a lover was found wanting because of poor brushwork.

A common early verse form was the *tanka,* arranged in lines of five, seven, five, seven and seven syllables for a total of 31. Verses were not rhymed and had no meter, but they almost always included a delicate reference to nature, as in a graceful *tanka* penned by Lady Murasaki and loosely rendered here: "Someone passes, / And while I wonder / If it is he, / The midnight moon / Is covered with clouds."

To be sure, five lines could be thought of as somewhat confining, although the range of possible imagery was wide. Longer poems did exist, composed by two or more poets in a sort of challenging game called linked verse. One writer penned the opening three lines of a five-line *tanka,* making them as self-contained as he could, whereupon another would demonstrate his skill by "capping" them to complete the *tanka* adroitly.

In time versifiers began extending the form, adding stanzas of two or three lines until hundreds or thousands of lines had been penned. Poems with more than 10,000 links were not uncommon; by the 14th Century the generating of such wonders had become a popular pastime not just in court circles but also among soldiers, priests and even ordinary citizens.

At length everyone wearied of the exercise and began focusing on just the opening three-line stanza of 17 syllables. By the beginning of the 17th Century the 17-syllable *haiku* had superseded the *tanka* as a popular verse form and had become a fixture of Japanese literary life.

Simplicity and the use of the most economical means to obtain an effect

Seventeenth Century painter and poet Matsuo Basho immortalized a roadside hibiscus in this scroll and added a verse that has the real flower come to an ignoble end: A horse eats it.

were the essence of *haiku,* and they revealed the influence of Zen Buddhism, which had been imported from China around 1200 A.D. (along with tea). Other Buddhist sects had won converts in Japan centuries earlier, taking their place beside Shinto, the historic Japanese "way of the gods" based on worship of nature. But while Amida and Kegon Buddhism stressed the necessity of having faith in something outside oneself, Zen Buddhism looked inward, with an emphasis on meditation and self-understanding *(page 148).* Through mental discipline, one could achieve enlightenment — which could come from any sudden perception.

Despite their apparent simplicity, *haiku* are anything but simple. Not only do many Japanese words have multiple meanings, but many words with widely divergent meanings are almost identical, so that the finest *haiku* can be interpreted many ways and may be overflowing with imagery. Many virtually defy translation.

But the best *haiku* succeed as much for what they do not say as for what they do. Words are deliberately omitted to heighten the effect and make the poem more evocative, as in the following: "The peaks of clouds / Have crumbled into fragments — / The moonlit mountain."

Not only is no connection specified between the clouds and the mountain, but the implications embodied in the *haiku* are to be supplied by the reader, in active partnership.

The "moonlit mountain" *haiku* was written by Japan's greatest poet, Matsuo Basho, who lived from 1644 to 1694. It was Basho who established *haiku* as the pinnacle of Japanese poetic expression, insisting that each verse embody both permanence and change

A KNACK FOR EXQUISITE PACKAGING

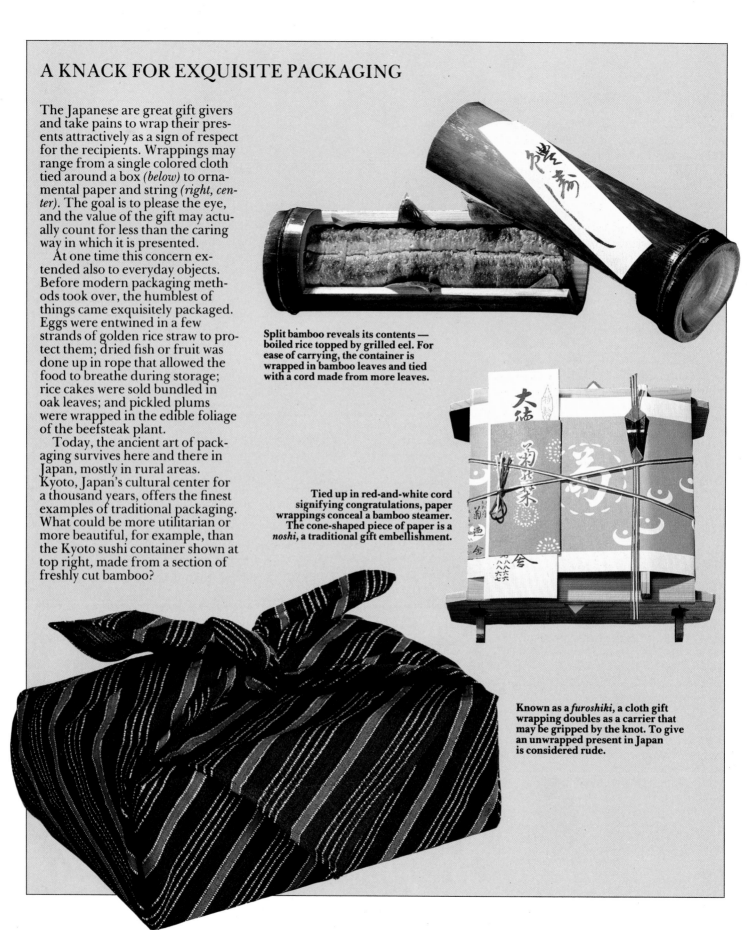

The Japanese are great gift givers and take pains to wrap their presents attractively as a sign of respect for the recipients. Wrappings may range from a single colored cloth tied around a box *(below)* to ornamental paper and string *(right, center)*. The goal is to please the eye, and the value of the gift may actually count for less than the caring way in which it is presented.

At one time this concern extended also to everyday objects. Before modern packaging methods took over, the humblest of things came exquisitely packaged. Eggs were entwined in a few strands of golden rice straw to protect them; dried fish or fruit was done up in rope that allowed the food to breathe during storage; rice cakes were sold bundled in oak leaves; and pickled plums were wrapped in the edible foliage of the beefsteak plant.

Today, the ancient art of packaging survives here and there in Japan, mostly in rural areas. Kyoto, Japan's cultural center for a thousand years, offers the finest examples of traditional packaging. What could be more utilitarian or more beautiful, for example, than the Kyoto sushi container shown at top right, made from a section of freshly cut bamboo?

Split bamboo reveals its contents — boiled rice topped by grilled eel. For ease of carrying, the container is wrapped in bamboo leaves and tied with a cord made from more leaves.

Tied up in red-and-white cord signifying congratulations, paper wrappings conceal a bamboo steamer. The cone-shaped piece of paper is a *noshi*, a traditional gift embellishment.

Known as a *furoshiki*, a cloth gift wrapping doubles as a carrier that may be gripped by the knot. To give an unwrapped present in Japan is considered rude.

— an unchanging truth as well as a fresh perception.

Born of a *samurai* family, Basho early rejected the warrior's way, choosing instead to live an ascetic life. He became a teacher of poetry in Edo (present-day Tokyo), and at first he was known as an expert in the composition of linked verse. Not until he was 35 years old did he write his first *haiku:* "On a withered branch / A crow has settled — / Autumn nightfall."

And several more years passed before he began turning out in quantity the verses for which he is venerated. Most of these resulted from a series of travels Basho made about the countryside on foot or on horseback, accompanied by friends or students — to whom he could be a stern taskmaster. Sometimes those who traveled with him would amuse themselves by composing linked verse, but Basho concentrated on writing an evocative travel diary interspersed with relevant *haiku.* The travel diary had long been a familiar Japanese literary form, but no one mastered it as did Basho.

As it happened, the emergence of Basho as a master of *haiku* was not an isolated phenomenon: Japan at the time was enjoying a vigorous renaissance in all the arts. Known as the Genroku period, and lasting from 1688 to 1704, the outpouring took place less than a hundred years after the Tokugawa shoguns had closed Japan off from the rest of the world. Isolated but thriving, the country enjoyed a cultural boom. Two forms of theatrical entertainment — *noh* and *kabuki* — were being offered, representing major contributions to the world of drama that continue to attract audiences even in the multimedia 20th Century.

The disciplined, severe form that is

noh theater today resulted in large part from the work of two men, father and son, who were patronized by the ruling Ashikaga shogun during the late 14th and early 15th Centuries. The father, an actor known as Kanami, regularized the drama's musical accompaniment by presenting it as a chanted, rhythmic narrative punctuated by stamping and turning. His son, Zeami, who was strongly influenced by the teachings of Zen, determined the mood of *noh* for all time by emphasizing quiet under-

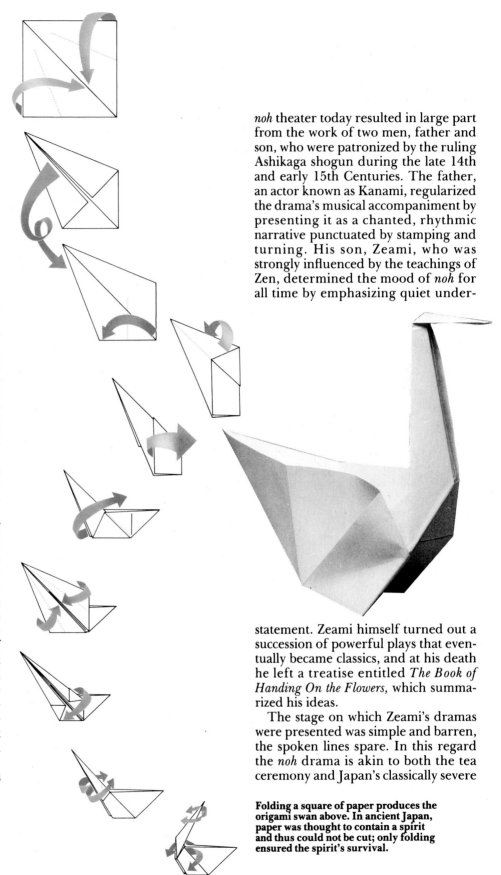

statement. Zeami himself turned out a succession of powerful plays that eventually became classics, and at his death he left a treatise entitled *The Book of Handing On the Flowers,* which summarized his ideas.

The stage on which Zeami's dramas were presented was simple and barren, the spoken lines spare. In this regard the *noh* drama is akin to both the tea ceremony and Japan's classically severe

Folding a square of paper produces the origami swan above. In ancient Japan, paper was thought to contain a spirit and thus could not be cut; only folding ensured the spirit's survival.

form of landscape design, both outgrowths of Zen.

In most *noh* dramas, as refined by Zeami, there are just two main characters: a principal actor and a secondary one. A handful of minor personages and a chanting chorus complete the cast. Masks are frequently used, but only the principal actor and the supporting cast may wear them. This sets the actors off from the secondary character, who must go without one. The masks heighten illusion. By tradition all the female roles are taken by men, and masks help them in this deception. In the same way, a young man playing the part of an old warrior is aided by his mask. *Noh* masks are infinitely varied and constitute an art form themselves, for many have been created by eminent artists.

Many of the plays are derived from ancient myths and legends. As prescribed by Zeami, five are presented at a performance, each with its own theme. Emotionally important scenes are in prose; the climaxes to these are in poetry. The poetry sections are punctuated by the stamping of the actors' feet and the drumbeats of the musicians — strict attention being paid by all performers to the rhythm of the words and the mood of the scenes.

The tone of these dramas is relentlessly serious and frequently tragic. The aim, said Zeami, is to reveal to the observer a Zen quality called *yugen,* literally "what lies beneath the surface" and is "obscure and dark." But *yugen* also connotes a beauty tinged with melancholy. "When notes fall sweetly and flutter delicately to the ear," wrote Zeami, that is the *yugen* of music; and the symbol of *yugen* is "a white bird with a flower in its beak."

By the mid-16th Century, *noh* dramas were being performed increasingly for the aristocracy, who alone could enjoy the subtleties and complications. Fifty or so years later, *kabuki* appeared — and has been a fixture of Japanese theater ever since.

In the newly emerging merchant class of the Genroku period, the lusty *kabuki* found a ready audience. Socially ostracized but with money in their pockets, the merchants and traders developed their own culture, gathering in the pleasure quarters of the country's three major cities, Kyoto, Osaka and Edo. In such quarters as Edo's notorious Yoshiwara district, "the Nightless City," entertainment was available not just in the green-shuttered brothels — though these were plentiful and many were extremely luxurious — but in every other pursuit, from musical performances to wrestling matches to poetry readings. The bustling subculture was known generally as *ukiyo,* a Buddhist epithet denoting the transience of life and translatable as "the floating world." And a key ingredient of the floating world was *kabuki.*

The first *kabuki* dancers were women who performed under the auspices of Buddhist shrines. One particularly talented and attractive shrine dancer, a priestess named Okuni, is responsible for giving *kabuki* its name. In 1603, she brought a troupe of young women to Kyoto, calling her act *kabuki,* which means "song, dance, skill." Okuni herself was somewhat bizarre; she often wore a costume of Portuguese-style trousers, an outlandish hat, a jacket and a crucifix, although she was not a Christian. But her troupe packed the crowds in, for the women were available to male patrons after the show.

Okuni interspersed the dances with short plays, some erotic; in one, she appeared in male attire as a customer seeking a prostitute, in another as a maiden emerging from her bath. *Kabuki* was clearly ideal entertainment for the floating world.

Okuni's dancers and their successors were so attractive, however, that fights over them broke out now and then. In 1629, the government banned women from the *kabuki* stage, and their places were taken by young males of beautiful appearance. But similar fights erupted, for these dancers were equally available to the customers.

therefore not express the synthetic ideal. The ideal woman can be expressed only by an actor." (In the early 1980s, one of Japan's leading *onnagata* was such an artist that aspiring actresses and real-life geishas studied his performances, seeking ways to refine their own femininity.)

In the eyes of the shoguns, *onnagata* and other actors were outside society — nonpeople, on equal footing with the courtesans of the Yoshiwara district and other denizens of the floating world. But what the stars of *kabuki* lacked in official recognition, they more than made up for in popular acclaim. They were the celebrities of their era, comparable to modern television and rock stars. Great actors became the founders of dynasties: Their names were passed to their sons or adopted sons and so on down through the generations. The inheritors were distinguished from their predecessors by the Japanese equivalent of roman numerals. One noted actor today is the seventeenth of his line.

Kabuki theaters themselves preserve a connection with the past in their layouts. The central feature is an elevated walkway called the *hanamichi* (or "flower road"), which runs through the middle of the audience. On it the stars make their entrances. Not long after the curtain has gone up to reveal a sumptuous setting, perhaps of a magnificent merchant's palace of two centuries ago, lights suddenly shine on the *hanamichi*. There, says one observer, will be standing "a warrior of immense powers, a courtesan of incredible beauty, a villain of unparalleled wickedness — figures from the world of superlatives who pass through our midst and make us feel exhilarated to belong to the same human race. A performance

They were outlawed as well, and since 1653 all *kabuki* roles have been performed by grown men.

With the disappearance of seductive females or males from the stage, *kabuki* had to resort to exciting drama and virtuoso acting to draw its audiences — and thus it has endured. The shift also gave rise to what was to become a central feature of the art: the use of female impersonators, or *onnagata*.

At first the ban on women performers was considered a handicap, but so great were the talents of the *onnagata*,

even when they were middle-aged men playing young beauties, that audiences were ready to believe they were more beautiful than real women. The *onnagata* achieved their illusion by concentrating on the inward qualities of beauty rather than its appearance, the abstraction of womanhood rather than its reality. Said one celebrated *onnagata* of the early 18th Century, "If an actress were to appear on the stage she could not express ideal feminine beauty, for she would rely only on the exploitation of her physical characteristics, and

FEASTS FOR THE EYE AND THE PALATE

The hallmarks of Japanese cuisine are simplicity and elegance. "Food should be prepared to do honor to the essence of the materials chosen," one master chef has said, and only the freshest of ingredients are used, for two important reasons. Japanese believe that their food must not only taste good, it must look good.

Every aspect of a meal may be a form of artistic expression. For example, the preparation and serving of the finest *sashimi* — raw sliced fish — constitute a dazzling ceremony known as *shikibocho*. The master chef, armed with a razor-sharp knife and two chopsticks, approaches a raw carp lying on a chopping block. He bows, then in a series of lightning moves, slices off head and tail, and chops and chips away. Finished, he holds up a string of tiny fillets, joined together in a chain, then reassembles the silvery morsels into the body of the fish. He bows again and leaves the room with an artist's stately pace.

Japan catches and consumes more fish and shellfish than any other country, and these are often eaten fresh and raw. Indeed, some Japanese prefer to eat shrimp when they are still alive and wriggling. The ritual is called *odori* (dance). A shrimp is pulled alive from a tank, gutted and prepared for eating in about five seconds, then grabbed by its wriggling tail, dipped in sauce and swallowed. Gourmets insist the flavor is infinitely better while the morsel is still "dancing."

An exquisitely fresh, delicately sliced sea bream, ready for immediate eating, lies on a stoneware plate garnished with pine needles, *nori* (seaweed) and *wasabi* (green horseradish paste).

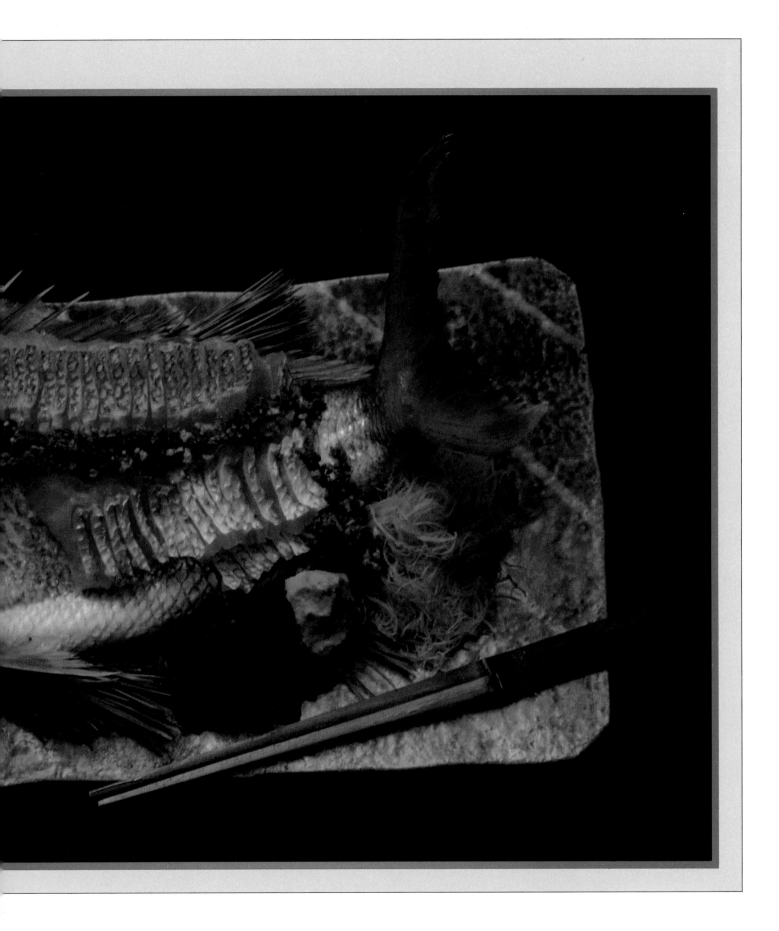

of *kabuki* causes most other forms of theatre to seem pallid."

The plays themselves may be melodramas, situation comedies or even tragedies that are Shakespearean in their psychological intensity. But if today they seem quaint to many, it should not be forgotten that they often reflected reality and contained social or political commentary, for the merchants who thronged the theaters relished any veiled criticism of the Tokugawa samurai who had looked upon them with such contempt.

One everlastingly popular play was based on an incident that actually took place at the beginning of the 18th Century and strongly influenced the entire island nation: A band of samurai whose master had been killed rose in revenge against the lord they believed to be responsible for the death. The play, which was translated and adapted into English in 1915 by the British poet John Masefield, has become an international favorite under the title *The Drama of the 47 Ronin (ronin* being masterless samurai).

Two techniques heightened the impact of early *kabuki.* One was magical stagecraft: The stage and runway abounded in trap doors, and a revolving stage was introduced in 1758, more than a hundred years before such a device appeared in European theaters. The other was the stylized acting. Audiences became accustomed to seeing the hero — flamboyantly costumed and elaborately made up — stirring a caldron brimming over with the heads of his enemies, or making a giant rat disappear in a puff of smoke. The most bravura acting, called *agagoto,* or "ruffian stuff," was likely to build up — as it still does — to a climax known as a *mie,* in which the actor struck an extreme

pose with a grimace on his face and his eyes crossed.

Such exaggerated realism could be found in yet another theatrical feature of the floating world, the puppet theater. Eventually known as *bunraku,* for a puppeteer named Bunrakuken who helped perfect the art in Osaka, Japan's puppet plays are like nothing else in the world. The puppets themselves are huge — two thirds life-sized — and their operators sit onstage in full view of the audience. The unlikely arrangement was no bar to success, for throughout the Tokugawa era, *bunraku* rivaled *kabuki* for public favor.

Descended from musical narrations offered at shrines and temples during medieval times, *bunraku* was at first presented with conventional puppets that were manipulated by hidden operators. The stories were based on heroic legends. As time went on, the puppets became larger and the manipulation was brought out into the open. Puppets grew to four feet in height, and each was worked by two men and finally, in the 18th Century, by three. Although two of the operators wore hoods, the principal manipulator not only was unhooded but was richly costumed, a practice that continues to the present day. Also fully visible onstage were the chanter, or narrator, and the musician playing accompaniment on the three-stringed *samisen.*

The puppets became highly complex as the number of their operators increased, and eventually it became possible to simulate agitated breathing, to move the fingers and eyebrows convincingly, and to make every gesture fluid and lifelike. More important, by turning its back on conventional realism, *bunraku* could focus on the sheer drama inherent in a play. As one ob-

server put it, the puppets made unreality the agent of the utmost reality. "The living actor," wrote the French poet Paul Claudel after seeing *bunraku,* "remains always a man in disguise. The marionette, on the other hand, has no other life or movement but that which it draws from the action. It comes to life with the story. The creature of wood is the embodiment of the words spoken for it."

Given such potential, it is not surprising that one of Japan's greatest dramatists, the 17th Century playwright Chikamatsu Monzaemon, switched from the *kabuki* theater to writing exclusively for *bunraku.*

Catering directly to his floating-world audience, Chikamatsu for the most part turned out domestic tragedies that were frequently based on actual events among the tradesmen and merchants of Osaka, where he had come to live. Many of his plays were centered on a socially unacceptable romance that might culminate in the double suicide of the lovers, a common enough occurrence in the pleasure quarters because, while sex was permitted, romance was not.

Such sensationalist works were wildly successful, and Chikamatsu created a new play every few weeks. His most popular *bunraku* drama, however, was a heroic, bloodcurdling work called *The Battles of Coxinga,* which ran for 17 months and was seen by an estimated 240,000 people — in a city whose population was less than 300,000. *Coxinga* was eventually adapted for the *kabuki* stage. Thereafter, *kabuki* plays were constantly borrowed from *bunraku,* and some *kabuki* actors even made note of the transference by acting in an artificial, jerky manner to simulate the movements of the puppets.

BUILDING ON THE PAST

At first glance, contemporary Japanese architecture may seem completely Western in appearance, but a closer look reveals the fundamental Japanese quality of *shibusa*. *Shibusa* is not just beauty, but the beauty of calm understatement, expressed with flair.

The density of Japan's cities and the chaos of their growth would seem to contradict the idea of *shibusa* as a force in Japanese architecture today. But working within the tight constraints of space, architects are achieving some of their finest effects, as in the building below. The serene interior matters more than the exterior.

Sharply geometrical, a Tokyo bank squeezed onto an awkward site faces a parking lot.

The windows overlooking the parking lot are deliberately opaque, except for one that frames a tiny view.

4

While *kabuki* and *bunraku* were vying for the attention of crowds thronging the Yoshiwara and other pleasure quarters, and while the *noh* drama was still playing to its devoted clientele, the floating world was giving rise to a form of popular graphic art that would, centuries later, excite critics in the West: wood-block prints.

The prints were designed by skilled

artists and printed in quantity to be sold on the street. They might show a *kabuki* actor, grotesquely made up, striking a *mie* pose; or a scene from a play with two star-crossed lovers contemplating suicide; or an elegant dandy surrounded by alluring courtesans in a luxurious teahouse. Many printmakers turned out complete sets of pictures of courtesans, which were sold as *bijin-e*, or "pictures of beautiful women" — the pin-ups of the era.

As time went on and the public gave indications of being ready to buy more, artists began expanding their subject matter. Traditional myths were represented, as well as birds and animals, landscapes and even contemporary

events. Some wood-block prints were embellished with finely wrought calligraphy, which on close inspection might be seen to embody incisive political commentary damaging to the shogunate that kept the floating world's society repressed.

At first toiling anonymously, wood-block artists by the end of the 17th Century had begun to sign their prints, and some have since then acquired international reputations. Torii Kiyonobu, for one, produced such bold, energy-filled posters for the *kabuki* that he and his descendants held a virtual monopoly on Japanese theatrical poster art for almost a century. Multicolored, vibrant prints with the richness of paintings were turned out by Suzuki Harunobu, who would use strong colors for figures but grays or olive greens for his backgrounds. His style came to be known as Edo brocade painting.

Such opulent graphics culminated in what is known as the golden age of Japanese printmaking, a 12-year period that lasted from 1789 to 1801. The star of the age was Kitagawa Utamaro,

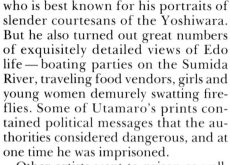

who is best known for his portraits of slender courtesans of the Yoshiwara. But he also turned out great numbers of exquisitely detailed views of Edo life — boating parties on the Sumida River, traveling food vendors, girls and young women demurely swatting fireflies. Some of Utamaro's prints contained political messages that the authorities considered dangerous, and at one time he was imprisoned.

Other artists went to prison as well, for the shoguns were becoming increasingly wary of what they saw as the corrupting influence of the floating world. By 1801, a system of censorship was in place. All prints had to be marked as politically acceptable by an official of the shogunate. Prints deemed decadent were restricted. Despite the censorship, however, two of Japan's greatest wood-block artists flourished during the first few decades of the 19th Century. Ichiryusai Hiroshige was a master landscapist, achieving subtle graphic effects in his delicately colored winter scenes and evocations of summer rains, autumnal mists and spring evenings.

Even more remarkable was Katsushika Hokusai, the greatest Japanese artist of the 19th Century. A man of enormous vitality who was given to grand gestures, Hokusai once delighted a crowd that had gathered for the unveiling of a public statue by taking the occasion to paint a mammoth portrait of a Buddhist patriarch. On a huge composite piece of paper that was laid out in the street, Hokusai made the portrait using brooms for brushes and ink held in sake tubs.

Hokusai was constantly experimenting with new styles. He was among the first of the major Japanese painters to make serious use of Western tech-

Moonlight Revelry, **a painting by Utamaro, the most famous artist of Japan's Golden Age (1789-1801), depicts courtesans at a seaside pavilion. Over the course of his highly successful career, Utamaro produced prints for no fewer than 52 publishers.**

niques of perspective. European artists admired him, and the Impressionists in particular were inspired by his technique. One of his 15 sketchbooks became available to them, and they were entranced by his delightful and variegated studies of farm women, magicians, animals, monsters, insects — every conceivable subject — all rendered in brilliant detail.

Although artists of the merchant class were rarely recognized by Japan's rulers, there is an often-repeated story that claims that one day Hokusai and another artist were ordered by the reigning shogun to produce works on the spot, for his amusement. When his turn came, Hokusai stretched out a long roll of paper on the floor, then took from a basket a live chicken. After coating the bird's feet with vermilion ink, he set it running across the paper. It left a trail of bright footprints as it went. Hokusai prostrated himself before the shogun and proclaimed the painting's title: *Autumn Maple Leaves Drifting on the Tatsuta River.* Luckily the shogun was pleased, and the artist's fame spread still further.

In 1823, when he was in his sixties, Hokusai began work on what would be his masterpiece, a collection of prints entitled *The Thirty-Six Views of Mount Fuji.* In these he went far beyond mere landscape depiction, for practically all of the prints show aspects of life in the country and use Fuji only as a refrain-like backdrop. The prints were endlessly inventive. One in particular astonished his Western admirers. Entitled *Great Wave off Kanagawa,* the print shows three small boats about to be inundated by massive breakers rearing up forbiddingly around them. Mount Fuji is only a tiny image in the background. The impression conveyed is one of demonic energy.

When Japan's course was altered so dramatically in the mid-19th Century with the influx of Western ways, woodblock printing was unable to compete with newer pictorial forms such as photography and lithography, and it went into decline, not to revive again until the 20th Century. The traditional dramatic arts narrowly escaped a similar eclipse. The *noh* drama, whose practitioners had subsisted largely through

allowances from the shoguns, seemed about to expire. That it did not was due partly to the enthusiastic endorsement of former U.S. President Ulysses S. Grant, who on a visit to Japan in 1879 was invited to see a performance at a diplomat's residence. Grant urged Japan's new rulers to preserve the art. Today *noh* continues to draw devoted audiences of connoisseurs. *Bunraku* puppets, though increasingly incomprehensible to Japanese youth, are protected and subsidized by the government as a national treasure and have their own adherents.

Kabuki has been more fortunate. Although its survival seemed in doubt for a while early in this century because of a dearth of trained principal players, interest has quickened in recent years. Now protected by the government, *kabuki* is still able to fill its 2,000-seat theaters — albeit often with theater parties and touring foreign groups. An all-star *kabuki* troupe that visited the United States in the early 1980s played to packed houses.

Nevertheless, dramatic forms like *noh*, *kabuki* and *bunraku* represent a distant if revered past, and do not receive any creative input from present-day Japanese artists and writers. Rather, the art forms absorbing some of the most imaginative and creative artists in Japan today are fashion, film and literature. In the world of international fashion, Japanese designers are revolutionizing the shape and form of clothing itself *(page 106)*, making a direct impact on the West in a way that most other manifestations of Japanese culture have not. And the once-vital Japanese film-making industry is showing signs of a renaissance after a quarter century of stagnation.

Although Japanese films have not

Japan's highest mountain, Fuji, stands outlined against the cloud-brightened sky in this wood-block print by Hokusai. The artist made 36 views of the volcano and issued them as a set. It proved so popular that he produced 10 more views.

4

been widely distributed in other countries, the Japanese have been making movies since the early days of the cinema. Japanese film makers were content at first to reproduce on celluloid memorable moments from *kabuki* or from ancient history. Starting in the 1920s, however, their films began to take on a distinctive aura, and in the years just before and after World War II, they earned well-deserved critical acclaim internationally.

One film genre, *shomin-geki,* dealt exclusively with lower-middle-class life. The pictures had a realism that was not evident in Western films of the same era. Japanese films run about two hours in length and are usually slower-paced than American or European movies. Often the camera lingers on a particular object or scene for minutes at a time, inviting the audience's contemplative thoughts. Above all, Japanese films are notable for conveying the atmosphere of a locale so penetratingly as to seem to go far beyond the limits of the screen itself.

Many Japanese films, indeed, are as severe, restrained and enigmatic as any *noh* drama or *haiku*—especially those of the late Yasujiro Ozu. Ozu's films, which deal with everyday relationships, were photographed entirely from the eye level of someone sitting on the tatami matting of a traditional Japanese room, the camera hardly moving at all.

Yet, just as *kabuki* stands in sharp contrast to *noh,* so have the Japanese also turned out their share of samurai films filled with zest and action. Some of the most remarkable of these have been the work of Akira Kurosawa, perhaps Japan's best-known and most accomplished director; indeed, Kurosawa has been called one of the world's finest cinematic creators.

LESSONS IN PURITY AND REFINEMENT

The tea ceremony, an ancient Japanese ritual, is considered a social refinement that women should master. Courses in its intricacies are taught nationwide — even, as the photograph at bottom shows, in a Tokyo department store.

The drinking of tea is only a part of the ritual. The ceremony involves the appreciation and contemplation of the various utensils used, of the tearoom's decor and any exterior views. Indeed, the ritual has been described by one Japanese as "an excuse for the worship of purity and refinement."

The tea is a bitter, green brew, whisked to a froth and consumed slowly and reverently, often with cakes or other delicacies. Cups and plates are deliberately mismatched. Some are new, others heirlooms, and each is to be enjoyed in its own right. Thus food is never allowed to cover a plate completely, since the plate may impart as much pleasure as the item it holds.

Tea-ceremony utensils fill shelves at Tokyo's Mitsukoshi department store.

The Mitsukoshi department store's tea master *(left)* watches a pupil perform.

Kurosawa first became known to movie-goers in the West not long after the end of World War II. The American Occupation forces administering the defeated land had demanded the making of films that would help the Japanese adjust to a less militaristic regime, and a spate of movies appeared that attempted to promote individuality and the rights of women. A few superior films emerged, and some of the best were remarkable indeed. The one that suddenly brought Japanese cinema — and Akira Kurosawa — to the world's attention was his *Rashomon,* which won the Grand Prix at the 1951 Venice Film Festival. Overnight, Kurosawa had become an artistic force to be reckoned with.

No one was more surprised at this than the Japanese film critics, who had not liked the film. The producing company, dismayed at their response, had not intended to send it to Venice and did so only on the urging of an Italian critic in Tokyo. But there is no mistaking the superiority of *Rashomon.*

A kind of psychological whodunit set in medieval Japan, the film explores a single event — involving a rape and murder — as seen by five persons involved in it. Its elliptical quality has fascinated audiences all over the world; five wholly different versions of the story leave the audience wondering which of the characters is telling the truth and chillingly makes the point that reality is subjective.

Kurosawa followed up this triumph in 1952 with *Ikiru,* the touching story of an elderly bureaucrat with terminal cancer whose yearning to accomplish something meaningful before he dies leads him to defy his superiors — a heretofore unthinkable act in Japanese eyes. Of his films, it is one of Kurosawa's two favorites. The other is *Seven Samurai,* which was released in 1954 and which many observers consider to be one of the finest examples of film art ever created.

Set during the height of Japan's feudal period, *Seven Samurai* tells the story of a band of masterless samurai, or *ronin,* who are asked to defend a remote peasant village from attacks by bandits. The *ronin* succeed in wiping out the bandits, but in so doing they demonstrate their own diminished usefulness to society, for it is the peasants who really emerge as the victors. The movie is in turn lyrical and thrilling, occasionally comic but more often sad. The samurai are lonely remnants of a dying world; as their value declined, one observer noted, "it was as if the spirit of Japan, like a candle in the dark, had suddenly gone out."

For the next two decades after the appearance of *Seven Samurai,* the candle of Japanese film making itself seemed on the verge of flickering out. Kurosawa, hamstrung by cautious studios looking for quick profits, was able to make only four films between 1965 and 1983. But there have been small signs of a revival. In May 1983, for only the second time since 1954, the top prize at the Cannes Film Festival went to a Japanese work. This time it was Shohei Imamura's *Ballad of Narayama,* a stark portrait of Japan's mountain people in the 1880s.

Despite a market dominated by young viewers whose tastes run to action and exaggeration rather than to psychology and subtlety, *The Ballad of Narayama* was a box-office smash. So were three other films playing at the same time: Kon Ichikawa's *Makioka Sisters* (about an upper-class family just before World War II), Masaki Kobayashi's *Tokyo Saiban* (a grueling four-and-a-half-hour documentary of the Tokyo war-crimes trials) and Nagisa Oshima's *Merry Christmas Mr. Lawrence* (a melodrama set in a Japanese prisoner-of-war camp in 1942).

While none of these film makers has yet gained the international stature of a Kurosawa or an Ozu, their films, as one respected Japanese film critic put it, "are neither flukes nor mutants." Rather, they mark a return to prominence by directors who have been working in movies for at least a quarter

4

A REVOLUTION IN FASHION

When Japanese designers first made a splash on the international fashion scene in the 1960s, they were regarded largely as a curiosity. Their creations, although original, were basically in the European tradition — tricky variations on conventional forms. No longer. Today some of the best Japanese designers have returned to their roots, creating a fashion revolution that has changed the shape and form of clothing itself. Disdaining the distinction between craft and art, they use native fabrics and weaves to turn out clothes that are intended for everyday use but are also things of beauty.

Issey Miyake, regarded by many as Japan's leading designer, works like a sculptor. With no predesigned sketch, he drapes cloth over the entire body and allows the collaboration of cloth and body to dictate the final shape.

What Miyake and other Japanese designers are trying to do, he says, is "peel away to the limit of fashion." Their clothes relax around the wearer, not enveloping or constraining the body, but rather exalting its freedom.

Designer Miyake crouches before a model wearing his "bird of paradise" jacket and skirt.

of a century. Moreover, these recent, ambitious projects continue to explore the society's traditions — rigorous self-discipline, honor, revenge — and they offer viewers the reassurance that the culture maintains its identity in spite of Western inroads.

Nowhere is this identity more vigorously proclaimed than in modern Japanese literature. In his *Thousand Cranes* and *Snow Country,* the late Yasunari Kawabata, a Nobel Prize winner in literature, addressed the theme of erotic obsession with the subtle obliqueness of a *sumi-e* painting. Yukio Mishima, perhaps the country's most celebrated novelist, was, by contrast, a writer of extravagant, *kabuki*-like sensibility. In such works as *Confessions of a Mask* and *The Temple of the Golden Pavilion,* Mishima harked back to the militaristic eras of Japan's past and denounced the self-indulgent society he perceived around him. In November of 1970, Mishima made the ultimate protest: After his attempt at a military coup d'état failed, he committed *seppuku* — ritual self-disembowelment, followed by decapitation at the hands of a member of his private "army."

The despair expressed by Mishima is emphatically not shared by Hisashi Inoue, one of the most prolific and successful writers in Japan — or in the world — today. The most celebrated of his 50-plus books is *Kirikirijin (People of Kirikiri),* an 834-page comic novel that sold more than 850,000 copies during its first two years. "I don't like *bonsai*ism," Inoue has said, in explaining his outsize narrative. "I think it is perfectly all right for some trees to grow big and wild."

Inoue, whom Japan's critics have dubbed the "magician of language" for his incessant wordplay, is not the only

internationally prominent novelist. Writers like Kobo Abe *(Woman in the Dunes)* and Kenzaburo Oe *(Hiroshima Notes; A Personal Matter)* regularly sell 150,000 copies of each book. Shusaku Endo's spare and elegant studies of Christian faith and martyrdom have made him one of the nation's most widely translated writers.

In addition, one Japanese expert has noted that the country's literary scene is showing a return to a tradition not witnessed since the era of *The Tale of Genji:* More and more women have taken to writing fiction. Perhaps the most respected among them is Taeko Kono; her novel *Revolving Door* deals with protagonists whose apparently ordinary lives cloak sadomasochistic and other pathological behavior. Yuko Tsushima examines the roots of family distress and false nostalgia in *A Bed of Grass.* And Taeko Tomioka, like Lady Murasaki a poet-turned-novelist, is celebrated for her unflinching investigations of social despair.

In a society where, as one literary

scholar has described it, silence is a powerful compulsion and writing an act of defiance — even for men — Japanese women writers have had to deal with double the social pressures that assail their male counterparts. The selfless submission prescribed for Japanese women by their culture is antithetical to the discovery or the creation of a personal writing voice. As one Japanese anthologist — herself a woman — has observed, "Women writers have needed great courage to surmount the many obstacles to their attempts at such self-assertion."

But this self-assertion, contrary though it may be to some Japanese traditions, is nevertheless fully in line with others. Lady Murasaki, for one, provides a role model of centuries-long standing. Moreover, the reentry of Japanese women into the literary arena signals yet another instance of the country's historical ability to adopt and adapt whatever the wind and the tide may bring to its shores — in this case, modern feminism. □

Doraemon, a robot cat, is Japan's best-loved comic-book character. More than 50 million Doraemon comics have been sold. In this strip, read from right to left, he receives birthday gifts, including a surprise, then retaliates by giving his friend one: the boy's fierce mother.

Tamao Yoshida is a master of *bunraku*, which features almost life-sized wooden puppets. The hooded figure is an assistant.

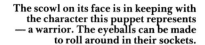
The scowl on its face is in keeping with the character this puppet represents — a warrior. The eyeballs can be made to roll around in their sockets.

The scowl on its face is in keeping with the character this puppet represents — a warrior. The eyeballs can be made to roll around in their sockets.

A GALLERY OF LIVING TREASURES

Nations pay tribute to their cultural idols in ways that tell a good deal about their people's values. Great Britain has its poet laureate, France its 40-member Académie Française. In the United States there are academies that honor illustrious writers, artists and scientists — as well as Halls of Fame for its athletic heroes.

Japan honors its most precious cultural assets in a unique way. As befits a nation whose heritage of artistic craftsmanship goes back many centuries, it has bestowed the title of Holder of Important Intangible Cultural Properties on about 70 living craftsmen, some of whom are seen here and on the following pages. The honorees receive a lifetime annual stipend from the government enabling them to exhibit, perform and teach apprentices who will keep the ancient crafts alive. But more important to them than any financial rewards are the psychic ones: Revered by all Japanese, from the Emperor down, they are regarded, and affectionately referred to, as *Ningen Kokuho* — Living National Treasures.

Irregular in shape and pitted with air bubbles, one of Toyozo Arakawa's cups displays the naturalness that is the hallmark of his work. Such cups are much sought after for use in the tea ceremony.

DISCOVERER OF A LOST ART

Out for a walk one day in 1930, Toyozo Arakawa, a painter, made a discovery that was to change his life. He had stumbled on the remains of a centuries-old kiln, used for firing a type of much admired antique pottery that no one had been able to reproduce. Stirred by his find, he determined to uncover the secrets of the vanished potters. He built a kiln on the same site and, through patient experimentation, began to recreate their lost techniques.

Today Toyozo Arakawa is one of Japan's leading potters. He occupies an old farmhouse in the hills and each day follows a stream to his workshop. There, often with the window open and the sun streaming in, he sets his potter's wheel in motion and allows the clay to take shape under the press of his fingers. After decorating and glazing the pieces, he fires them in the single chamber of the reconstructed kiln, which is dug partially into a hill to catch the breezes. He tends the fire for 10 days, gauging from the color of the smoke and flames when the pottery is at last ready.

Toyozo Arakawa leans on a stick in his garden. Designated a Living National Treasure in 1975, he says of himself: "I surround myself with the beauty of nature to create."

Decorating a bowl, Arakawa uses loose, spontaneous strokes. He fires only what he likes, when he likes, lighting his kiln once a year or so.

A MUSICAL BRIDGE TO ANCIENT JAPAN

Fumiko Yonekawa is the grand old lady of Japanese music. She is considered by many to be the country's foremost practitioner of the koto, a stringed instrument — imported from China — that had become a permanent feature of Japanese court music by the 17th Century.

The daughter of a samurai family, Miss Yonekawa learned to play the koto when she was three. Her sister, who was blind, had begun to study the instrument, a traditional undertaking for sightless Japanese, and Fumiko went along to the lessons. She has been playing ever since, and in 1966 she was named a Living National Treasure.

Today the koto is the favorite instrument of tradition-minded Japanese. Since 1917 Miss Yonekawa has taught hundreds of pupils, including her two adopted daughters, who are also brilliant musicians and teachers. Once a year, former students and those taught by her apprentices come to her studio to pay homage and take part in a recital. On rare occasions, Miss Yonekawa still gives personal recitals. "It is through reaffirming the past," she says, "and passing on the traditions to the future, that my fingers remain strong and limber enough to play."

Watched by her cat, master musician Yonekawa practices her instrument, something she still does six hours a day. The koto, about six feet long, has 13 strings of tightly coiled silk or nylon stretched over a slightly arched body made of paulownia wood.

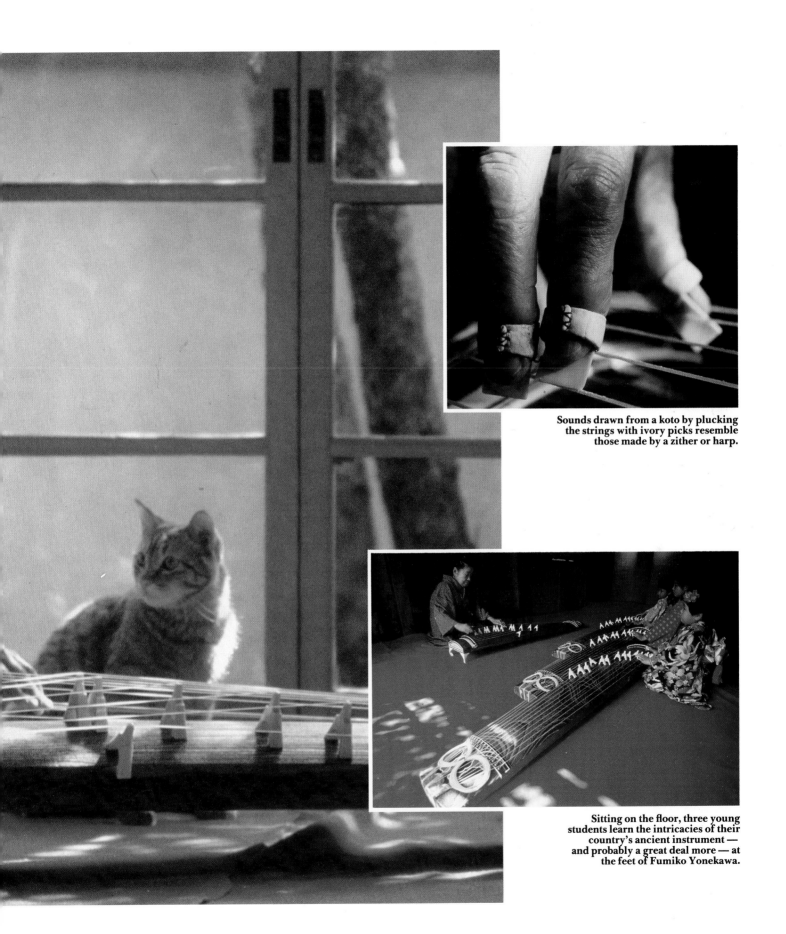

Sounds drawn from a koto by plucking the strings with ivory picks resemble those made by a zither or harp.

Sitting on the floor, three young students learn the intricacies of their country's ancient instrument — and probably a great deal more — at the feet of Fumiko Yonekawa.

113

UPDATING AN ANCIENT CRAFT

In Kyoto, which was the capital of Japan for a millennium and is still its spiritual center, Kako Moriguchi has been making elegant, exquisitely patterned kimonos for more than 50 years, using dyes and techniques that date back to the 17th Century. It is an intricate process, taking as long as six months. First, the design is sketched on a kimono of plain, undyed silk. Then the garment is taken apart, and the design is outlined with a dye-resistant paste that is allowed to dry before the area is colored in. The procedure is repeated again and again, the paste being washed out each time. When finally the drying is finished, the strips of cloth are sewn back together.

What emerges is a sumptuous gown but also, in vibrant color and composition, a work of art. "My methods are old," says Moriguchi, "but I want my designs to be new. Unless tradition has a growing, spiritual base, it becomes static imitation."

The outlines of a flowered pattern are delicately applied with a special paste that keeps the dyes from bleeding into adjoining areas.

114

Kimono designer Kako Moriguchi calls
this pattern Early Spring. Like
heirlooms, his kimonos are handed
down from mother to daughter.

Sprinkling gold dust, Moriguchi,
a Living National Treasure since
1967, completes a kimono design.
His four apprentices spend 10 years
living and working with him.

A DYNAMO FUELED BY HUMAN ENERGY

Nikon. Casio. Seiko. Yamaha. Nissan. Toyota. Sony. Panasonic. Sharp. Pioneer. Toshiba. The brand names are everywhere, an outpouring of consumer plenitude that sweeps the globe and includes everything from cameras, calculators and digital watches to motorcycles, grand pianos and automobiles. Virtually all of the video cassette recorders that have been sold in the United States and Europe since the device's invention have been made by Japanese companies. Japan has also produced a huge proportion of the world's transistor radios, tape machines and stereo sets.

Western scientists devised the technology that spawned today's high-speed computers and electronic gear, but such Japanese firms as Hitachi and Matsushita have manufactured huge numbers of the silicon memory chips that make it possible for these machines to function. The industrial robot was pioneered in the U.S. back in the 1950s, but in the 1980s an executive from Detroit or Minneapolis wanting to automate the company's production lines might well go to Tokyo to find out how it is done.

Japan's industrial vitality is one of the wonders of the modern world, a trillion-dollar-a-year cornucopia of quality goods and services that accounts for a full 10 per cent of the world's economic output. Only the United States and the Soviet Union produce more, and Japan's economy has been growing faster than those of either superpower.

Japan has achieved this economic growth against extraordinary odds. At the end of World War II, so many of the country's factories lay in smoldering ruins that industrial production had plunged to one seventh of the 1941 rate. Massive doses of American aid — $400 million a year in the late 1940s — were needed just to feed and clothe the destitute population. Those few factories still in operation were set to turning out the most rudimentary goods — shoes fashioned from scraps of wood, kitchen pots stamped from soldiers' discarded steel helmets. The notion that the Japanese would soon be competing successfully with the advanced industrial powers of the West seemed an impossibility.

The Japanese had other formidable odds to overcome. No other industrial nation is as barren of essential resources. Virtually all the crude oil that, after refining, is consumed in Japan's homes, cars, factories and power plants must be shipped in from overseas, along with 90.7 per cent of the natural gas Japan uses and 81.8 per cent of the coal. Japan is the world's largest steelmaker except for the Soviet Union but, having no iron mines to speak of, it must also be the world's largest importer of iron ore. Japan gets most of its lead and copper ores, bauxite, wool, cotton and lumber from overseas. "We are very different from the rest of the world," one Japanese executive has

Shinto priests perform a ceremony of purification in front of a reactor pressure chamber, heart of a new nuclear power plant. The rite is intended to ensure worker safety.

5

said. "Our only natural resource is the hard work of our people."

Despite wartime destruction and an irremediable paucity of natural resources, the Japanese have quietly and purposefully made their nation into the world's third-ranking exporter of manufactured goods. During the two decades between 1960 and 1980, Japan's gross national product burgeoned an average of 7.45 per cent each year, outstripping the GNP growth rates of every other industrialized nation.

This astonishing resurgence has sent shudders of perplexed alarm through business and government circles in the West. "If technology is looked on as the ability to get good, working products out the factory door," lamented one American executive, "I think the Japanese are taking over." How, many envious Westerners have asked, do the Japanese do it? Will Japanese products continue their aggressive invasion of Western markets? Will Japan come in fact to dominate the world's economy?

The effort to answer these questions has spawned a minor growth industry in studies of Japanese business methods. These studies have resurrected some old myths about Japan, have punctured some others and have given rise to new sets of often contradictory theories and interpretations.

Some of the theories explain Japan's postwar success in terms of the island nation's supposedly low wages and feudalistic labor practices: Many Western businessmen picture Japan as a transistorized anthill, a nation of faceless drones willing to toil long hours for little reward. Another theory has it that the Japanese, poor at inventing things for themselves, have succeeded largely by pirating the technology of others, and then swamping world mar-

kets with low-cost imitations. A more sophisticated scenario has Japanese businessmen and government officials working hand in glove to manipulate the economy — a sort of Japan Incorporated, which promotes key industries, creates cartels, erects import barriers, rigs prices, dumps merchandise on foreign markets and generally conspires to gobble up more than its fair share of world trade.

There is some truth in all these theories — along with large amounts of exaggeration and misconception. For example, Japan does have some import tariffs, but in recent years they have been no higher than the trade barriers erected by most nations. What the Japanese have done on occasion is make it extremely difficult, through complex inspection procedures and other restrictive measures, for foreign competitors to do business in Japan. For example, every automobile imported into Japan must be partially disassembled so that customs agents can determine whether all serial numbers check with those on the shipping documents. This expensive, time-consuming process naturally helps deter the entry of foreign vehicles into the Japanese market.

The failure of foreign firms to crack the Japanese market can more often be traced, however, to the ineptitude of the would-be exporters than to Japan's trade barriers or other restrictions. Foreign firms have seldom troubled to familiarize themselves sufficiently with Japan's particular tastes and circumstances. The Japanese have taken such pains. "For 20 years I went to the U.S. to sell my company's products," Hisashi Shinto, President of Nippon Telegraph and Telephone, has said. "We devoted our major effort to knowing your government regulations, our customers'

practices and requirements. Every Japanese company has operated the same way. Why don't American firms follow this practice?"

There is also a mixture of truth and falsehood in Western charges that a generally low wage scale has allowed Japan's industries to undersell foreign competition. In the larger Japanese companies, in fact, wages have risen remarkably in recent years, reaching levels at least comparable to those in Western Europe. Smaller Japanese firms, on the other hand, have been forced to pay less well to keep costs down.

As for the notion that Japan has flooded world markets with cheap and imitative goods, it is true that the Japanese have borrowed many ideas and techniques from the West. It has become increasingly difficult, however, to dismiss as mere mimicry Japan's excellent cameras, sports cars and other top-quality exports. In any case, the value of Japan's exports, although impressive, has represented in recent years a scant 12.5 per cent of the nation's total GNP. As an overseas trader, Japan has ranked well behind Great Britain (20.4 per cent of GNP in 1983), West Germany (25.8 per cent) and Canada (23.5 per cent).

The issue of government aid to business presents another mixed picture. It is true that the Japanese government has subsidized the growth of some industries and helped them enter foreign markets. But the government has never given any special boost to either the auto or consumer electronics industries, which have been the most successful of all.

The reasons behind Japan's postwar economic miracle are more complex, and far more interesting, than many theories suggest. The reasons are deep-

AN IDEA OLYMPIC

Though they may place great demands on their employees, Japanese businesses are not all work and no play. Toyota, for example, sponsors an Idea Olympic, a pleasurable annual exercise in creativity, begun in 1976, that encourages its personnel, as one senior engineer says, "to tinker and produce something original."

Of the company's 50,000 workers, more than 1,000 engage in the competition. A recent winner, a drafting supervisor for the auto maker's maintenance department, came up with the motorized swing-on-wheels at right. It serves no other function than to amuse.

This low-slung electric vehicle has a steel frame with bicycle wheels attached.

ly rooted in Japan's history and are as unique in character as the Japanese themselves. The Japanese have long demonstrated a remarkable ability to adapt the technologies of other countries. Pottery making came from China by way of ancient Korea, as did silk growing. When Japan rapidly modernized itself in the late 19th Century, emissaries fanned out through Europe and the United States to learn the rudiments of science, medicine, engineering and finance. Today, Japanese businessmen devour Western technical journals, and the overseas offices of large Japanese corporations and trading companies spend so much of their time gathering information that they have been accused of operating like an industrial intelligence network. A recent study claimed that Japanese electronics firms have spent as much as $30 million a year to staff listening posts in such places as California's so-called Silicon Valley, heartland of the U.S. computer industry.

Japanese companies have also ac-

quired new technology through outright purchase, spending more than $10 billion between 1950 and 1980 to buy foreign patents and manufacturing rights. This may be an enormous sum, but it is far less than would have been the total if the Japanese had developed the same technology from scratch. The expense has been worth it in other ways. By waiting until a new technique or device has been tested elsewhere, the Japanese have generally avoided the cost of false starts — and have been able to choose from among the most promising innovations.

There has been nothing slavish in Japan's thirst for foreign expertise, however. Whatever has been borrowed has been transformed, often improved upon and usually streamlined and miniaturized into something uniquely Japanese. In 1953 Akio Morita, co-founder of the Sony Corporation, paid a U.S. firm, Western Electric, $25,000 for nonexclusive rights to manufacture the transistor, an American invention that was then thought to have only

limited commercial use. The resulting transistor radio — handsome, compact, conveniently portable — helped turn Sony into one of the leading electronics firms in the world, with an enviable knack for coming up with inventive new products such as the ubiquitous Walkman radio. "The nature of business is to make your own product obsolete," Morita has declared. "If we don't do it ourselves, we know our competitors will do it for us."

In the effort to stay ahead, Japanese companies not only have bought the rights to much foreign technology, but also have spent huge sums on their own "R and D" — research and development. Japanese firms in recent years have poured an average of 6 per cent of revenues into R and D, as opposed to only about 1 per cent for U.S. companies. As a result the number of patents issued yearly to Japanese nationals by their government has begun to outstrip the number granted by the U.S. patent office to American individuals and firms, and to outpace patents issued in

5

England and France by a ratio of 7 to 1.

Still another reason for the worldwide appeal of Japanese exports has been the demand for excellence in the nation's domestic marketplace. More than 85 per cent of all goods made in Japan are earmarked for home consumption. "Our target is not some other country," one electronics executive has explained; "our target is ourselves." To which a U.S. economist has added: "The Japanese have had success in foreign trade because of their competitiveness at home."

To win out in a land that has 11 competing automobile companies — more than any other nation — and where such electronics giants as Sony and Hitachi must battle a succession of eager upstarts requires both a high level of inventiveness and rigid cost controls. Price wars are endemic. Any manufacturer unable to streamline his operation and cut overhead will be forced out of the market.

While they fight to trim expenses, the competitors must constantly strive to upgrade quality, for Japanese consumers have become famous for their choosiness. When shopping for refrigerators they automatically run a hand across each surface to make sure that screwheads do not protrude. Automobile buyers check the upholstery for proper stitching, examine the paint job inside the trunk and open the hood to inspect the welds.

This insistence on nothing but the best may seem even more remarkable in light of Japan's past reputation as a purveyor of shoddy merchandise. Before World War II, during the country's first major industrial push, a raft of hastily built items with "Made in Japan" labels began appearing in inexpensive stores in the West. So prone were these trinkets to instant breakdown that several exporters, hoping to boost sales, set up shop in the town of Usa, in Kyushu, so that they could stamp their wares "Made in USA." Japan's first postwar products were hardly an improvement. The predecessors of today's high-performing Japanese sports cars were notoriously tinny and unreliable; the 1948 prototype of the first Datsun designed for export had a top speed of just 35 miles an hour.

The turnaround came, in part, through the wholesale importation of Western technology. Engineers from the Radio Corporation of America arrived to advise on the manufacture of television sets. Textile experts from Du Pont helped speed Japanese production of synthetic yarns.

To follow up these lessons in Yankee know-how, the Japanese sought help in improving their manufacturing techniques. In 1950 they invited a statistician from the U.S. Census Bureau, W. Edwards Deming, to lecture on a method for statistically monitoring the quality of a company's products. The Japanese seized upon Deming's message. Control of quality became a national passion. Japanese manufacturers began to engage in furious statistical battles, each company trying to prove that it had achieved the lowest defect rate. A national award, appropriately called the Deming Prize, has been given annually since 1951 to reward improvements in the caliber of products or business procedures.

Going U.S. manufacturers one better, most large Japanese firms have upgraded and updated the old suggestion box by organizing quality-control teams — small groups of workers that meet regularly to review their part of the operation and come up with ideas for improving it. Employees have taken up this challenge with the utmost seri-

ousness. Toyota has received as many as 500,000 such suggestions from groups of staffers in a single year — at a saving to the company of $230 million. There has also been an important dividend in worker dedication. Says Toru Iijima, a production-line foreman at the rival Nissan Motor Company: "If I hear that a car produced by Nissan has any problems, I feel personally guilty."

It seems astonishing that Japan has been able to combine its quest for quality with one of the world's highest production rates, but such has been the case. A Japanese factory hand simply turns out more goods per hour than his American or European counterpart. Devotion to the task accounts for some of this, but the deciding factor is the reliability and sophistication of Japan's industrial plant. Japanese manufacturers invest heavily and continuously in the most advanced equipment available. Nissan, for example, follows a "scrap-and-build" policy in which its factory equipment is constantly being upgraded and, in effect, is replaced every four to five years. By 1981, the company's highly automated assembly lines, attended by only 35 workers each, were disgorging 350 car bodies every eight hours — several times the production rate of the most efficient Western auto makers.

Japan's steel industry is another case in point. A few years ago American steelmakers protested that the Japanese were dumping underpriced steel on the market and threatening to put them out of business. The fact was that Japanese steel firms had cut their costs by installing such state-of-the-art technology as continuous casting, and using computer-controlled production systems and furnaces that speed smelting by superheating the steel with blasts of

oxygen. The resulting efficiency helped Japanese firms to cut labor costs per ton of finished steel to less than half the cost in any Western country, some of which were still employing an open-hearth technique 30 years out of date. Despite having to import their iron ore from overseas, the Japanese could ship finished steel priced 20 per cent lower than the competition's.

The most dramatic Japanese innovations have been in the field of robots, amazing devices that have caused a giant leap forward in factory automation. An industrial robot is essentially a metal box equipped with one or more mechanical arms, the box bolted to the factory floor. The machines can assemble parts, do welding or even — depending on how they are programmed — work in conjunction with adjacent machine tools to cut, drill or bend metal parts before attaching them.

Robots are fast, clean, tireless, undemanding, uncannily precise. Further, they can often do jobs at a far lower cost than the human labor they replace. Fanuc, a leading manufacturer of robots, machine tools and electric motors, has two plants at the base of Mount Fuji, with production lines that operate completely on their own, without benefit of human hands. In both, robots toil unattended through the night; during the day small groups of human employees maintain the robots and assemble some of the components the robots have made. Both plants function with a tenth of the human labor force that would be required to run a conventional operation. One of the plants — need it be said? — produces parts for more robots.

Such futuristic operations have begun to cause alarm among Japanese workers. They wonder what employ-

Rather than a room, guests get a cubicle at this Tokyo hotel. A favorite of businessmen seeking to save money, such cheap hotels offer bed, mirror, TV, radio and alarm clock, all in a space less than seven feet long and five feet high.

5

ment will be left for them, as an exploding robot population takes over more and more manufacturing tasks. One answer offered by farsighted Japanese businessmen and politicians has been that Japan must increasingly devote its attention to what could be called intelligence industries, to building ever more complex computers and other thinking machines. Leave the hard, repetitive or dangerous jobs for the robots, and train the human work force for the increasingly subtle tasks that the future will require.

The installation of robots and other forms of plant rejuvenation on the Japanese scale requires vast amounts of capital spending. Fortunately for Japan's businesses, the country's ingrained financial habits favor the accumulation of the needed funds. The Japanese over the years have been the world's most conscientious savers, squirreling away nearly one fifth of their annual disposable incomes into Postal Savings Accounts offered by the government, and other accounts offered by commercial banks. They save partly out of natural thrift, partly because the Postal Savings Accounts have been a smart buy, with the annual interest on the first 3 million yen (about $13,000) tax-free. Indeed, many Japanese have sought to escape the tax bite on additional interest by setting up accounts in the names of wives and children, often at a number of different post offices. By one estimate, there were 318 million such accounts in 1981, more than three times the number of Japanese adults.

All these annual savings — more than $40 billion a year in Postal Savings Accounts alone — have acted as a powerful engine for capital development. A company seeking to upgrade its factories borrows the needed money, either directly from the government or after it has been channeled by the government into the banking system. Either way, improvements tend to be funded through loans rather than, as in the West, through the sale of shares. Under this system a company must pay interest, of course, and this adds to its operating costs. But in return it gains a remarkable degree of freedom in managing its affairs.

It is this freedom, in the opinion of many economic analysts, that has been one of the most important ingredients in Japan's steady industrial growth. Western companies must continually account to their shareholders, who tend to look for steadily increasing profits and dividends. A Japanese firm is under no such constraint. Since whatever shareholders it has are limited in number, and usually include the bank that extends the loan, the company must simply clear enough to pay its employees and cover its debt. The result, according to one Western businessman, is that "the Japanese have patient money. They can afford to take the long-term view."

Passing up the quick payoff, Japanese companies plan 5, 10, even 20 years ahead. Nippon Electric started making silicon memory chips for computers in 1958; it was 1971 before the chips showed a profit. Since 1971, however, Nippon Electric has become one of the biggest and most successful chip makers in the business. The bottom line in Japan is not so much profits as growth and market share — the ability to seize an ever-larger portion of the market from competitors.

The long-term outlook of Japanese business has been carefully fostered by the policies of the government. So close at times has been the cooperation between businessmen and bureaucrats that European and American critics have had reason to accuse the nation of being a kind of industrial cabal, ruled by a close-knit power elite of 3,000 high-level bankers, politicians, industrialists and government officials, all apparently intent upon world economic domination.

From the mid-1950s into the 1980s, the government has in fact been unabashedly probusiness. All but one of the national elections held since World War II have been won easily by Japan's conservative leadership. The Liberal Democratic Party, which, despite its name, has been staunchly conservative, has maintained a comfortable majority in the Diet, or parliament, easily outdistancing its closest rival, the labor-oriented Socialists. The other political parties — the Clean Government Party, the Communists, the Social Democrats and a scattering of smaller groups — have carried so little weight that the Japanese sometimes say that theirs is a "one-and-a-half party system."

The LDP's continuing hegemony, bolstered in part by generous campaign contributions from the business community, has engendered the kind of long-term stability in which business thrives. Further stability — and a probusiness bias — has come from the country's highly effective civil service, which wields most of the real day-to-day powers of government.

Officials at Japan's government ministries, recruited from the top of their class at the country's leading universities, represent a national elite of intelligence and ambition. It is they who usually draft the legislation presented to the Diet for approval, who set priorities and who generate as well as imple-

THE SEARCH FOR A WONDER WORKER

Japan, more than any other country in the world, has turned to robots to increase its industrial productivity. At the Nissan Motor Company, one of Japan's leading car and truck manufacturers, 90 per cent of car-body welding is being done by mechanical drones that are tireless, never grow bored on the job and can be repaired or replaced when they break down. Just 150 Nissan robots turn out 1,300 cars a day, a feat that would require twice as many human workers.

Close to 80,000 industrial robots fulfill a variety of functions throughout Japan today, and their numbers are growing. More than 100 companies now either make or sell them. And the government encourages manufacturers to invest in them by offering subsidized loans and tax write-offs to interested businesses. In addition, it has earmarked $150 million for the development of an "intelligent" robot.

Scientists have already evolved prototypes that can walk, climb and grasp. Their next step is to come up with robots that will see, talk and follow commands as well. The Japanese Industrial Robot Association predicts that within a few years the technology will have become so advanced that robots will be used on a "massive scale," to do everything from spraying fertilizer to cutting lumber.

When set in motion, this antique robot serves tea. But since it can carry only one teacup, it is more toy than machine — a far cry from the Japanese robots of today.

A robot known as "Waseda legs" (named for Tokyo's Waseda University) takes its first steps forward. One day it may help the legless to walk.

A computerized, four-fingered robot arm plays Schumann on an electric organ in a laboratory. The inventors hope to equip it with an "eye" that will enable it to read sheet music.

Descending a staircase, a robot uses sensors on its "feet" to determine the height of individual steps.

A blind man follows a seeing-eye robot. Automatic sensors guide it, warning of obstacles; but since the device is unable to hop up and down curbs or read traffic lights, its usefulness is still limited.

ment policy. The national budget, for example, is prepared by bureaucrats at the Finance Ministry, who do not take kindly to attempts by the Diet to readjust the figures. Ministry staffers have been heard to grumble that the budget "is not a political matter and politicians should not interfere with the government." But for all the considerable infighting that quietly occurs between various ministries and the people's elected representatives, most issues are resolved in the time-honored Japanese manner—through consultation leading to consensus.

The consensus has been aided by a clubbiness that extends throughout the upper echelons of government, politics and industry. Not only the top civil servants, but also virtually all of the leading politicians and businessmen belong to an old-boy network united by a common education at the best universities. Consider the bonds between the Ministry of International Trade and Industry (MITI) and the business sector it is empowered to regulate. MITI officials, like their counterparts in large corporations, enter straight from university and remain until the customary retirement age of 55. But on quitting the

Ministry, most senior officials take up key posts in industry as consultants or as company directors—a process jokingly called "descent from heaven." A few venture into politics. The resulting close-knit fabric of personal relationships has created a rare unity of outlook and purpose.

MITI has remained the favorite target of Japan Inc. critics—and its influence in charting the direction of the nation's economy has in truth been considerable. By channeling funds to enterprises of its choice, providing loans for expansion and grants for research, it has spurred the growth of certain industries, enabling them to compete in international markets. It has developed standards for manufacturers and set depreciation rates for new plants and equipment. Entire industries have burgeoned under MITI's care; steel, shipping and petrochemicals were all nurtured by money and expertise from Ministry planners.

But for all its supposed clout, MITI has worked its marvels with a remarkably light touch. Whereas Western governments habitually issue edicts regulating business practices, MITI has taken a more generalized approach. It has

analyzed market trends and then attempted, often through personal persuasion, to nudge businessmen into the most promising areas.

Conversely, when a particular industrial sector has appeared to be declining, the Ministry has brought its leaders together to effect an orderly cutback. Such was the scenario in the 1970s when oil prices soared, causing a drop in world demand both for crude oil and for new supertankers in which to carry it. This situation inevitably caused a recession in Japan's once-vigorous shipbuilding industry. MITI convened the company presidents and together they worked out a schedule of prices and production quotas that allowed the industry to shrink without causing serious harm to any one company. Jobs were saved, and production facilities were smoothly diverted to other uses.

Business usually listens when MITI speaks, but sometimes it does not. In the mid-1950s the Ministry decided that the country's leading auto makers should join forces to design a compact "people's car" similar in concept to the German Volkswagen. The auto makers quietly but firmly resisted the idea, and the proposal never came to a vote in the Diet. Later, thinking the auto industry overcrowded, MITI sought to discourage new entries and tried to promote mergers among the existing firms. One industrialist who outspokenly defied this policy was Soichiro Honda, the founder of Japan's leading motorcycle company.

Stubborn and flamboyant—his plain speaking had already earned him the nickname of "Old Man Thunder"— Honda hardly fit the stereotype of the consensus-prone Japanese businessman. And he was a habitual risk taker. Having seen his first airplane as a boy

Celebrating the Emperor's birthday, a flag-waving crowd assembles before the Royal Family just outside the Imperial Palace. According to Japan's Constitution, the Emperor derives "his position from the will of the people with whom resides sovereign power."

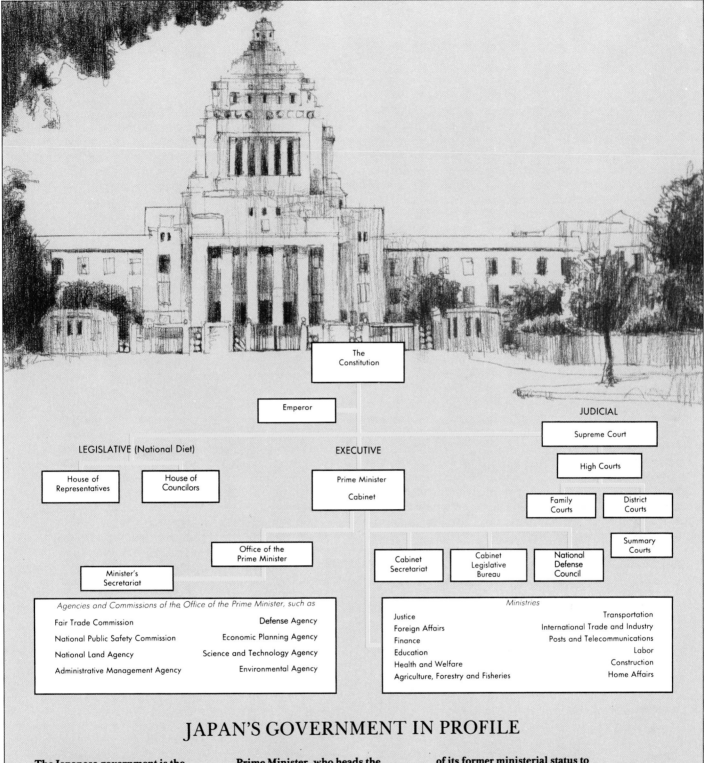

The Constitution

Emperor

LEGISLATIVE (National Diet)

EXECUTIVE

JUDICIAL

Supreme Court

High Courts

House of Representatives

House of Councilors

Prime Minister

Cabinet

Family Courts

District Courts

Summary Courts

Office of the Prime Minister

Minister's Secretariat

Cabinet Secretariat

Cabinet Legislative Bureau

National Defense Council

Agencies and Commissions of the Office of the Prime Minister, such as

Fair Trade Commission

National Public Safety Commission

National Land Agency

Administrative Management Agency

Defense Agency

Economic Planning Agency

Science and Technology Agency

Environmental Agency

Ministries

Justice
Foreign Affairs
Finance
Education
Health and Welfare
Agriculture, Forestry and Fisheries

Transportation
International Trade and Industry
Posts and Telecommunications
Labor
Construction
Home Affairs

JAPAN'S GOVERNMENT IN PROFILE

The Japanese government is the product of the 1947 democratic constitution. The Emperor, who has a symbolic function only, appoints a Prime Minister designated by the popularly elected National Diet. The Prime Minister, who heads the Cabinet, appoints and can dismiss his 12 Cabinet ministers. The office of the Prime Minister supervises the various governmental agencies (including Defense, which was stripped of its former ministerial status to curb the military's influence).

The Diet consists of a House of Representatives and a House of Councilors. The House of Representatives is the more influential body.

of eight in 1914, he promptly took a bicycle from his father's repair shop in the small town of Hamamatsu, fitted it with bamboo "propellers" and raced around the village terrorizing the neighbors. When he was 15 years old he dropped out of school and moved to Tokyo, where he apprenticed himself to an auto repair shop. Six years later he went into business for himself. Borrowing money wherever he could and rounding out his journeyman's skills with night courses at a technical high school, Honda was soon making piston rings as a subcontractor for Toyota. As a hobby, he built and raced his own sports cars.

During World War II Honda devised machine tools for fashioning airplane propellers, cutting the production time per unit from seven days to just half an hour. After the War he built his first motorcycle. By the early 1960s his internationally popular Super Cub cycles were bringing more money into Japan than the overseas earnings of either Toyota or Nissan.

The freewheeling Honda characteristically took MITI's automotive edict as a personal affront. "Are the bureaucrats trying to block our plans to build cars?" he ranted. "We'll show them!" And so he did. At the 1962 Tokyo Motor Show, he unveiled a light-duty truck and a prototype sports car, both cobbled together at record speed to escape a MITI deadline that would in effect have kept him out of the car business.

Once in, Honda swiftly produced another sports car, a small coupe and a minicompact. His first popular car worldwide was the Civic, which shortly began to give the Volkswagen Beetle stiff competition in the U.S. and elsewhere. By 1978, Honda had sold his millionth car in the American market; within five years his plants were turn-ing out more than a million vehicles a year. By then the company's founder had ostensibly stepped down from day-to-day control, assuming the title of "Supreme Adviser." But quiet retirement was not a part of Honda's character. "Because I love the company," he admitted, "I occasionally allow myself to say a thing or two about its operation."

Mavericks such as Honda are unusual in Japan — and therefore add a welcome color and sparkle to the corporate scene, which tends to be as monochromatic as the blue business suits worn by most executives all over the country. However, it is the wearers of these suits and their employees, more than volatile geniuses on the Honda model, that have made Japan so formidably successful. Careful decision making, tireless attention to detail and long hours on the job have been essential ingredients of the postwar economic miracle.

The reputation of the Japanese for dedicated, uncomplaining toil has become a modern legend. Like any other nation, Japan has its rebels and dropouts and dreamers. But generally, in the board room and on the factory floor, Japan is a nation of workaholics. In small factories especially, and in the mom-and-pop stores that are ubiquitous in Japanese neighborhoods, the workers labor long and hard. Employees in small workshops assume they will be at their benches five and a half or six days a week. Only in the largest industries has the work week been cut to 40 hours, and even there, intense, purposeful activity prevails at all times.

Corporate managers and government bureaucrats are often even more dedicated. A Western diplomat, called one night to an urgent 2 a.m. meeting at Tokyo's foreign ministry, was astonished to find long lines of taxicabs still parked outside each of the nearby government buildings, waiting to ferry home late-toiling officials. Nor were the drivers all dozing at their wheels; many were busily flicking specks of grime from their fenders with huge feather dusters, in some strange ritual of postmidnight zeal. "In Japan work is a ceremony," writer Ichiro Kawasaki has noted. "For the Japanese worker, life and job are so closely interwoven that it cannot be said where one ends and the other begins."

Various reasons have been put forward to explain the national addiction to labor, including the once hardscrabble farming so many Japanese had been forced to do on tiny plots of land. A chief motivation surely is a pervasive desire for group approval. Laziness in Japan is looked upon, as it was among the Calvinists of the West, as a dire moral lapse. "If the other members of your group work hard and you don't," explained shipping executive Yoshiya Ariyoshi, "you will eventually be ostracized. And being excluded from the group is the most appalling thing any Japanese can imagine."

The leaders of Japan's larger companies, aware of this need to belong, have urged their workers to think of the firm as a close-knit community, almost a family. With the blessings of Japan's unions, they offer their employees what have been called the "three sacred treasures." The treasures are, starting with the most important, a virtual guarantee of lifetime employment, promotion by seniority, and a union shop.

Lifetime employment means simply that: The large Japanese firms fire no one unless they find themselves in the most dire financial trouble. Even if an employee's job becomes redundant, every effort will be made to find the worker another slot within the company.

Festooned with "ribbons of shame," a young executive at a managers training school near Tokyo stands before his peers and enumerates his weaknesses. Such truthtelling sessions are supposed to build character and confidence.

When a business recession compelled Nippon Steel to shut down one of its furnaces near Tokyo, the company promptly set up an agricultural subsidiary and put its furnacemen to work raising cattle.

Many workers in the U.S. and Europe would probably view such blanket security as an invitation to slack off, to coast along until retirement. Both the Soviet Union and China, where workers are assigned to jobs on a long-term basis, have had problems with boredom and shoddy workmanship. Not so in Japan. Given the national craving for group acceptance, the typical Japanese company inspires an almost tribal sense of loyalty.

In return, the corporations exercise a parental concern for the welfare of their personnel. As Isamu Yamashita, chairman of Mitsui Engineering and Shipbuilding, once put it, "In today's Japan, companies like ours are the new communities, and their managers have a responsibility to create conditions in which people can enjoy a community life." And all employees are constantly assured that their contribution counts.

"All of us, every one of us in Japan," another businessman has declared, "believe that the rise or fall of our organization rests on the individual shoulders of each one of us."

Closely akin to lifetime employment is the second sacred treasure — an entrenched seniority system. Each employee moves up through the ranks in strict progression according to age and length of service, much like the grade-by-grade advancement of a student through school and college. Hiring occurs just once a year, usually in April. All new recruits arrive en masse, and an elaborate ceremony marks the event, with welcoming speeches by top management and the distribution of company badges. Then comes a period of training and indoctrination. Newcomers may be sent on religious retreats to Zen temples, or to commando-style survival schools where, in the interest of character building, they go on punishing hikes through the mountains or recite *haiku* poems while standing under icy waterfalls.

The training period usually lasts for six months, but it can be longer, depending on the category in which a new employee is hired. Every new arrival, whether fresh from trade school or carrying a college degree (and thus destined for a post in management), shuttles from job to job within the company, learning new skills and gaining insight into company goals and methods.

Eventually each of the college graduates is assigned to a section, the basic white-collar work unit. There the young manager-to-be takes his place — and most managers are men — at the foot of a double row of adjoining desks, becoming the lowest person on the team. For the next 30 years or so he will move up the corporate ladder, desk by desk and pay hike by pay hike. As he gains seniority he will become an assistant section chief and then a section chief — at which point he sits at the head of the row of desks, like a host at a dinner table.

A number of sections, each with its own tight cluster of desks, are lodged in a single large room, and together they make up a department. With time the employee may be raised to department head. There he normally comes to rest, surveying his domain from a solitary desk at the front of the room, until retirement, usually at the age of 55. Each move in this long progression has occurred according to a fixed schedule. Very rarely has a junior employee been jumped ahead of a superior. Only in the last dozen years or so of his career will an executive receive promotions or pay bonuses beyond those given out to his classmates.

To an outsider this system may seem unbearably rigid and stifling — and a few cracks in the system have recently appeared. Some talented junior executives have jumped from one company to another, lured by the possibility of swifter promotion. Executive recruitment specialists — whom Americans call "headhunters," long a fixture of the Western business scene — have appeared in Japan to help firms spot promising managers in the ranks of their competitors. In Japan they are called *heddo-hantaa.*

Most executives, however, stay with the company they joined originally. Within the seemingly rigid corporate system, there is a degree of flexibility. Certain sections and departments are more desirable than others, and the more promising workers find themselves assigned to these. Because each section operates as a team, a talented junior member may in fact exert far greater influence than his rank would suggest. His abilities will be quietly noted and remembered. Then, if he pursues his career with tact and zeal, he may, upon reaching the normal retirement age, be asked to stay on as an executive in the stratospheric reaches of upper management.

His less able classmates will not have been neglected, however. Because the large corporations are extremely choosy when hiring in the first place, their employees tend to be generally capable and intelligent. When in the climb up the corporate pyramid someone begins to stumble, he is simply assigned to one of the less vital departments. But he receives the same pay increases as his contemporaries, and matters will be so arranged that he never has to undergo the embarrassment of being forced to report to a younger man. Face is thus saved and corporate harmony preserved. Even older employees who have been shed in the retirement process may continue to serve, either as part-time consultants or on

the staff of a company subcontractor.

The third sacred treasure is the union shop. Large, industry-wide confederations have never caught on in Japan except among government employees, such as teachers, and in a limited number of other fields. In the world of business, each major firm has its own labor organization. There is a Hitachi union, a Sony union and so on. The result is a remarkably easy working relationship between labor and management. Japanese unions can be raucously demonstrative, to be sure. Each spring there is the *shunto,* or spring offensive — a period with huge rallies, snake dances, harangues, derisive placards and burnings in effigy. Although the *shunto* is largely show, it does serve as a reminder to management that the workers are organized — and it lets off a lot of steam besides.

The real bargaining meanwhile goes on quietly in executive suites. There the union leaders sit down with company representatives and work out a deal. "Everything depends on dialogue and trust," says Yoichi Takahashi, former head of the 77,700-member workers' association of Hitachi Ltd. "What is

good for the company is good for the union. The workers know that their labor is what makes the company prosperous." Owing to this cooperative attitude, there have been few strikes. In 1981 Japan lost only 14 workdays per 1,000 employees because of labor unrest; in the same year Britain lost 200 and Italy 583 per 1,000.

A seamless harmony in fact appears to govern virtually all aspects of corporate life, and especially the unique manner in which Japanese businessmen reach decisions. No individual ever seems to make them. Instead they appear to emerge on their own, as if by spontaneous generation, from lengthy processes of consensus building. Conflicts are submerged in the effort to find agreement.

A specific idea may emanate from anywhere — from the board room, from the production line, from a junior member of a subsection. But before any action is taken — even, indeed, before a formal proposal is drawn up — everyone who will be affected will have been assiduously canvassed and a seemingly endless series of small gatherings will have been held, with the par-

ticipants carefully sounding out one another's views.

When everyone involved has had his say, the appropriate management committee holds a formal meeting. The decision that emerges has long since been arrived at.

The consensus process is cumbersome and time-consuming, but it provides stability and cohesiveness; everyone concerned can support the result wholeheartedly. Similarly, every issue is treated to exhaustive discussion, preventing any new departure from being taken in unwise haste. As one observer has noted, "Problems in Japan often disappear by being talked to death." And when a decision is finally reached, it can be put into effect with startling rapidity.

This harmony, and the lifetime security offered by the three sacred treasures, govern life in the large companies, the blue-chip corporations whose trademarks are known around the world. Yet the industrial giants employ only about 30 per cent of all Japanese workers. The other 70 per cent labor for smaller firms — independent enterprises that employ 300 workers or fewer. Many of these firms act as subcontractors that supply components for the giants, as Honda once did for Toyota. Others are back-room operations that make everything from dolls to kimonos to plastic toys, all generally sold in local markets. These smaller firms account for more than one half of the country's industrial output.

Few small enterprises can afford to treat their employees with the same lavish paternalism offered by the giant corporations. Workers are often hired on a part-time basis, and even regular staffers generally earn only 60 to 70 per cent of the top industrial wages.

Nor do they enjoy many fringe benefits. There are few pension plans, no company housing, no company limousines for executives; indeed, the only manager may be the hard-pressed owner himself. And there is no lifetime employment.

Adding to these uncertainties is the hold that many of the large corporations maintain over their subcontractors. The big auto makers, for example, buy fully two thirds of their components from outside suppliers, thus saving the salary and inventory costs of producing the parts themselves. Because they are usually the sole buyers of any particular workshop's output, the auto makers can practically name their own price. Furthermore, during business slow-downs they can cut back their own expenses by reducing orders to their subcontractors. The smaller companies thus bear the brunt of any economic downturn. "A big company won't push any of its subcontractors over the edge if it can help it — but it will push him right up to it," one veteran Japan-watcher has observed.

The outlook is not entirely dismal for small-scale entrepreneurship, however. The general vitality of Japan's economy helps mitigate the perils. The demand for components runs high. Japanese consumers have money to spend, and they use much of it to buy the output of small local firms. One such small-scale operation has prospered for seven generations. This is the copperware shop owned and run by the Tamayama family in Tsubame City, a bustling provincial town 150 miles north of Tokyo. The Tamayamas and about 20 workers fashion superb copper cookware by hand in a large workshop located behind the family dwelling. Their output is small, and the

business grosses at most $500,000 a year, but better-off Japanese treasure the superbly made Tamayama pots and it seems likely that the family will be able to continue in the business for another seven generations.

Many other family firms survive and even prosper among the giants of Japanese industry, offering steady employment to a significant proportion of the work force. With the national employment rate topping 97 per cent, most minibusinesses have more trouble with finding able workers than with having to let people go. Farmers, retirees, unmarried women, mothers with grown children can all usually pick up extra income at a nearby factory or workshop. Many of them do. Others may take jobs at one of Japan's 1,673,000 retail shops, among them the mom-and-pop neighborhood stores at which Japanese consumers do a good deal of their shopping.

So tight is the labor squeeze, in fact, that some small manufacturers have turned to automation — just as the industrial goliaths have. One such producer, who makes plastic parts for watches, conducts his entire operation with three injection-molding machines and one robot, set up in a shed in his yard. He rents his electronic employee from Japan Robot Lease — said to be the world's first robot-leasing company for small businesses — for about a tenth of what it cost him to pay the four workmen he once employed.

Few small entrepreneurs get rich at such endeavors, but with the amazing vitality of Japan's economy, and the seemingly unlimited horizons opened up by its move into high technology, the chances are that some of them will. If so, their companies will become the Hondas and Sonys of tomorrow. □

Long-distance telephone operators exercise their spring prerogative: going on strike. The Spring Labor Offensive, known as *shunto*, involves 80 per cent of Japan's work force. Through unified action at this time of year, unions score regular wage gains.

A geisha instructs a pupil in the art of serving tea. Before she can become a geisha (the word means "cultivated person"), a girl like this must be taught dance, song, conversation, flower arranging and the tea ceremony, an education that takes years.

THE PRESSURE TO BE JAPANESE

A first-time visitor to Japan would likely conclude after a week of strolling — or rather jostling — through Tokyo's crowded streets that the Japanese are running with all possible speed away from their old ways of life to embrace a heterogeneous new culture, a bizarre mix of European and American influences combined with Japanese elements. The strident tones of British rock bands blare from record stores. The modish young strut in the designer jeans seen in New York, London, Paris and Rome. Quasi-Western bars offer haven in many downtown blocks, and the prestige drink for those who can afford it is Scotch or brandy.

The visitor would also find many Japanese as passionate about the Yomiuri Giants, the Nippon Ham Fighters or the country's other professional baseball teams as any baseball fan in the United States. The British-American game of golf has become such a craze in Japan that successful businesses gladly ante up $100,000 initiation fees for their managers to join the country's top private clubs. The Japanese, in short, appear to be determined to become the most cosmopolitan of all peoples, making a new culture from the best — or at least the most popular — fashions, fads, games and ideas offered by alien Western cultures.

This appearance, however, is profoundly deceiving. True, the Japanese passionately desire to keep up with the rest of the world. But emphatically they do not wish to join it. The Japanese are unique, and most of them want to stay that way. They remain an island people, almost as distinctive psychologically as they were before the arrival of Commodore Perry's black ships in 1853. They are, in a sense, a homogenous clan. The majority share the same essential beliefs and cultural values, as well as the same manners. Frenchmen born in Burgundy and Provence — or Englishmen from the Midlands and London — differ far more from one another than do Japanese brought up 1,000 miles apart on distant islands of their archipelago. Their ideal citizen is one who fits into Japanese society with a minimum of friction.

The agencies that turn a Japanese child into this ideal Japanese adult are the family and the nation's demanding and utterly uniform system of schooling. Both family and school hammer home the belief that society, the group, is more important than any individual, and that belonging to a group is essential for one's well-being.

The mother has responsibility for almost all the child-rearing tasks in Japanese households. Although many Japanese mothers today augment the family income with part-time jobs that take them away from home during some of the day, a majority remain full-time housewives at least until the children are well on in school. Their methods of child rearing differ markedly from those in Western countries — and re-

6

quire an amount of energy and dedication that defies comparison.

The typical Japanese *mama* devotes virtually all her time and attention to her children, seldom leaving them with a nursemaid or even with grandparents. When they are very young, she constantly entertains them with stories, songs and peekaboo games. She holds and fondles them, bathes with them and picks them up the moment they cry — or the moment before they cry. At bedtime the mother does not simply put her children to bed, telling them to go to sleep, but lies down with them until they doze off. Weaned late and fed when hungry, the Japanese boy or girl spends the first years of life in a cocoon of warmth and comfort. A Japanese mother, as one observer has put it, "tends to shrink her whole life to the dimensions of the child's world."

The small size of most Japanese homes serves to tighten family bonds. There is simply not enough space to give each child a separate room or even bed. Infants sleep with their mother, and older children sleep together. Everyone eats, plays, studies and works in the same confined area.

The Japanese have turned this physical necessity into a way of teaching cultural values. Propinquity demands self-restraint and cooperation. Individual whims and desires must be suppressed for the good of all. The Japanese mother also teaches the child that the family offers the only real protection from the terrors and dangers of the outside world. Many Japanese are keenly aware that the environment is potentially hostile, and this pervasive insecurity is passed on to the young. Only in the mother and the family, the child is told, is there protection from such dangers. One of the most effective threats a Jap-

anese mother can utter to an unruly youngster is to say she will lock the child out of the house. Keeping a Japanese child inside is no punishment at all.

The importance of the group is reinforced in other, more public ways. In Japan a child's birthday is accorded relatively little importance. For centuries, by Japanese custom, children were considered to be age one when born and to turn two years old on the following New Year's Day — in lock step with every other child born during the preceding year. This custom is breaking down somewhat, but many Japanese parents still adhere to the old system. A Japanese mother who has a baby in December, for example, will tell the neighbors her infant is *futatsu* (two) if asked during the next January, even though the child may be less than a month old. There is a certain logic to this; the infant is, after all, in the second calendar year of its existence.

Some younger parents today, influenced by Western customs, occasionally have birthday parties for their offspring, but such events are considered less significant than the children's festivals or rites of passage that are celebrated nationwide. The most colorful of these is the *Shichi-go-san*, the 7-5-3 Festival, held each year in November. On this holiday Japanese girls who are seven, boys who are five and toddlers of both sexes who are three years old are dressed in their finest clothing and taken to a Shinto shrine to thank the deities for allowing them to reach those ages and to request future blessings.

On May 5 every year, all Japanese boys take part in the Boys' Festival, the observance of which is marked by symbols of manhood drawn from Japan's martial past — banners, swords and miniature sets of ancient armor, for ex-

ample. Girls celebrate on March 3 with the Doll Festival, when dolls depicting the imperial court are displayed in almost every home that has a daughter.

One result of all these lessons in togetherness, reinforced by the extraordinarily close bonds between mother and child, is that most Japanese children are remarkably polite and well behaved. This can amaze Western visitors who assume that the seeming permissiveness of Japanese mothers must produce spoiled children. What such outsiders fail to appreciate is that because she coddles and coaxes her children, the Japanese mother seldom needs to exert any formal discipline. The children, it turns out, want to please and obey such an understanding and utterly protective figure. Punishments for infractions of household rules are virtually unknown in Japan.

Taught cooperation and imbued with the desire to please the mother, Japanese children easily absorb the values and ornate behavior patterns of Japanese society. Strapped to his mother's back, a small Japanese boy finds himself bowing as she bows — a quick nod to a store clerk, a deeper bow to a neighbor, repeated bows where some special obligation is acknowledged. He thereby learns naturally that the intricate forms and gradations of Japanese etiquette are based not on general courtesy but on specific relationships.

Later, should that same young boy act up in public, his mother will point out children who are behaving properly and warn the miscreant that everyone will stare at him if he continues his pranks. This teaches the twin fears of shame and ridicule, which are fundamental social controls in Japan.

From all this early training, Japanese children acquire two important traits.

CELEBRATIONS FOR THE LIVING AND THE DEAD

Bearing a portable shrine, men wend down a glowing Tokyo street during Bon, the lantern festival.

The Japanese love festivals, and there is hardly a time of year — or place, for that matter — without one. *Matsuri,* as festivals are called, are occasions for joy, and many have been celebrated annually for hundreds of years. Most are religious in nature, and they always involve a procession of some sort *(above),* the centerpiece of which is a *mikoshi,* or ornamental shrine.

One of the most popular *matsuri* is Bon, the lantern festival, held in summer; it has been celebrated ever since Buddhism was introduced into Japan, more than 1,000 years ago. Though its theme is death, Bon is not lugubrious in tone. It is a time when gifts are exchanged and ancestors are believed to pay visits to the living.

In preparation for the three days of Bon, houses and cemeteries are spruced up. On the first night of the festival, families carry white paper lanterns to the graves of their loved ones. When they arrive home, the members participate in a meal that may include all the favorites of the departed; they may even address the spirits.

On the third and last day of Bon, cakes of glutinous rice are laid out on the family altar to cheer and sustain the dead on their return to the spirit world. And to help them find their way back, lanterns are lit outside houses and fires are made.

But perhaps the most touching act is the release into lakes, rivers and streams of hundreds of little boats, each carrying a lighted candle that illuminates printed messages such as "service for the myriads of souls in the other world." Often a priest or a family member will add the names of the departed to the pieces of paper aboard the boats. Gradually the waters fill with the little craft, which sparkle as they are rocked by breeze and current, and then disappear, one by one, into darkness.

6

One is called *amae,* which can be translated as a profound and long-lasting need for the sort of warmth and approval the mother has provided. Boys especially — because they are traditionally more indulged than their sisters — will try to find *amae* again throughout their lives, often by establishing dependent relationships with other family-like groups and with new mentors.

The other trait is respect for authority. The early acceptance of the mother's word as law blends smoothly into later acceptance of authority in school — and a lifelong tendency to accept the values of society as a whole.

It is fortunate for the Japanese child that he or she does accept the authority of teachers when school-time arrives; success or failure in school will have a decisive effect on what sort of a life that child will lead as an adult. In no other country does so much depend on academic achievement.

Japan is essentially a classless meritocracy. The status, power and wealth a person may attain are, to a large extent, determined not by inheritance or family background, but rather by success in school — or more specifically, by success in a series of competitive examinations. Children take exams to qualify for the best grammar schools, then for the top high schools. Then they take a final series of exams that determine whether they will be admitted to one of Japan's more prestigious universities — or any reputable university at all. The schools and universities pay little attention to teachers' recommendations or to a student's extracurricular activities, leadership qualities or personality. Everything is decided by how diligently the applicant has studied — and by how readily the acquired knowledge can be applied at exam time.

The pressure to succeed in these exams, especially the last set, is immense. For a modern Japanese, the rank and reputation of the university one attends settles everything once and for all. The blue-chip companies and the top government ministries hire future managers almost exclusively from Tokyo University and a few others, which form the Harvard and Yale, or the Oxford and Cambridge, of Japan. Admission to one of these institutions puts a young Japanese on what former U.S. Ambassador to Japan Edwin Reischauer has called the fast escalator to the top.

And there is virtually no other way to climb on it. Only in rare instances do people get a second chance in Japan, and there are few opportunities for a college dropout to catch up later. Self-educated successes are rarer still. It is little wonder that the Japanese have a term for the period during which a student faces the crucial tests: *shiken jigoku,* or "examination hell."

To help their children navigate the system, Japanese families disrupt their lives to an astounding degree. Mothers especially expend enormous effort on the task of getting their children into and through the best possible schools. Indeed it is expected of them. A mother who misses a Parent-Teacher Association meeting must hand in a written note explaining her absence. She is expected to send her children to school well groomed and armed with both nutritious lunches and all the necessary books and supplies. Any failure along these lines may elicit a complaint from the school. If a child is sick, the mother may go to school herself, to sit in class and take notes so that the child will not fall behind.

When the children return home from school, most mothers are there to greet them. The Japanese press periodically deplores the plight of the nation's *kagi-ko,* or "key children" — those who carry house keys and must let themselves in after school because their mothers work. There are not a great many *kagi-ko* in Japan; the outcry is raised because the idea of a child entering an empty house is utterly abhorrent to the Japanese.

In the evening, the mother will sit with her children, encouraging them to do their homework. In some homes the studying child need merely press a buzzer to have Mama pad in silently with a cup of tea and a snack. She sharpens pencils, explains difficult parts of the homework if she can — and always stands ready to administer a quiz or a drill. Most important, she guards her studious offspring from outside noises and distractions; there have been reports of mothers taking violent revenge on noisy neighbors.

As the time for one of the crucial exams nears, the mother involves herself in determining strategy — which exams the child should take and how to prepare for them. From books, magazines, special TV programs, and extensive consultations with school authorities and other mothers, she researches all the options and weighs them against her child's strengths and weaknesses. There are even special courses she can take to teach her how to find the right strategy. She is often the one who waits in line long hours to apply for each exam, because the applicant cannot spare that time away from the books.

The fierce maternal devotion all this preparation involves reflects the fact that in Japan a mother's status and sense of achievement depend in large measure on her children's academic success. "Nurturance is her job and her

Prayers on sticks — offered by a student named Tokiko — implore the god of the Fushimi Shrine in Kyoto for help in passing her university entrance exam. Such ready-made prayers can be purchased at shrines.

children are her primary product," one authority has explained. "A mother whose child wears the uniform of one of the prestigious high schools is proud and secure." A child's failure, however, brings shame and disgrace.

But of course the greatest pressure is on the student. All sports, hobbies and other leisure activities are put aside as the exams near. Every waking hour is devoted either to regular schoolwork or to studying for the exams; sleep is cut back to four or five hours a night. Some educators, critical of the system, say that students become zombies during this period, losing all the spontaneity and eagerness of youth.

It is mostly boys who face this pres-sure; few Japanese girls are encour-aged to consider serious, lifelong ca-reers. But girls do not get off scot-free: for them, admission to a top high school or university represents a ticket to a "good" marriage. It would be un-thinkable for a male graduate of one of the best universities to marry a woman with no university education at all, and a man loses status if he weds a woman whose academic credentials are signifi-cantly inferior to his own. If that does happen, the woman may be snubbed and humiliated by her husband's family and friends. The converse — a well-educated woman marrying a man with lesser academic credentials — is regard-ed in Japan as absurd.

SHINTO: A RELIGION ROOTED DEEP IN NATURE

Shinto is Japan's native religion. It is a synthesis of ideas, attitudes and customs that over the course of two millennia has helped shape the Japanese mind. Unlike Christianity, it does not celebrate a founder; nor does it have a sacred book like the Bible. Shinto, the Japanese say, "is caught, not taught," passed from one generation to the next.

A fundamental Shinto belief is that the gods *(kami)*, humans and nature were born of the same parents and thus are all related. People have a mission in life. It is not only to fulfill the ideals and hopes of their forebears in their own lives, but to love and nurture their offspring so that these may realize in turn the ancestors' aspirations.

Shinto shrines, considered the dwelling places of the *kami*, are invariably places of beauty so that worshippers may feel close to nature and the divine and commune there with the dead.

Enveloped in mist, the buildings and other structures of a Shinto shrine stand among sacred trees.

The *torii*, a symbol of the Shinto religion, represents a gateway that sets off the everyday world from that of the spirit. Traditionally *torii* have been built of wood, but some are of metal and a few are even concrete.

Dippers and a basin of clear water stand outside the entrance to a Shinto shrine. Worshippers, in an act of purification, rinse their mouths and pour water over their fingertips before entering the holy precincts.

A fox, considered the messenger of the rice god, wears a bib provided by a worshipper seeking the god's favor. Rice cakes, like those at right, are among the offerings left at shrines.

Wooden tablets bearing inscriptions are, in fact, prayers left at a shrine by suppliants. Among the messages are some from single men and women seeking divine help in finding spouses.

A sacred rope of straw guards against entry of evil spirits into a shrine, while the paper ornament dangling from a branch *(above)* is an offering. According to some, the ornament symbolizes the jewels used to lure the mythical sun-goddess from a cave to which she had retreated with her light.

6

The only children with ambitious parents who escape examination hell are those fortunate few who gain entrance to elite private elementary and secondary schools. These schools, which are generally affiliated with prestigious universities, require applicants to take qualifying examinations, too — even for entry into kindergarten in some cases. But once accepted, the students — who are among Japan's most intellectually gifted — merely have to keep up with their regular schoolwork and pass nominal exams to be assured advancement to the next level. The pace is fast, but at least the students are freed of the burden of *shiken jigoku* and can better enjoy extracurricular activities and sports programs.

One reason the examinations are so hellish is that there are no set standards for passing or failing. Therefore, not even a brilliant student can say to himself, "All right, I've learned enough of this to pass." Someone else out there may have learned more, so every student must grind away without letup; each school has a limited number of openings each year, and it simply counts down from the top of the test ranking and admits that number.

Further pressure comes from the fact that the Japanese educational system puts great emphasis on memorization. Most authorities agree that this tendency can be traced to the complexity of the Japanese writing system. To become literate, a youngster must master nearly 2,000 Chinese characters plus two sets of phonetic symbols that are used with them. Only by endless repetition can the student acquire the most basic of educational requirements, the ability to read and write.

The habits learned in language study tend to color the educational process.

History lessons consist largely of memorizing names and dates. Science studies emphasize the mastery of formulas rather than individual inquiry.

For help with all this memorization — and for bolstering weak areas — many students facing the examination grind turn to Japan's proliferating cram schools. These commercially run schools, called *juku*, range from tiny establishments holding classes in a teach-

er's home to large institutions in buildings equipped with up-to-date teaching aids and kitchens to feed the students. Some especially apprehensive students attend *juku* early in the morning before their regular school begins, then go back in the afternoon to stay through the evening. Some of the larger cram schools even provide dormitories for those who study until it is too late to go home. It is not uncommon for the big-

ger *juku* to bundle their students off to resorts for 12-hour days of study during the brief school vacation periods.

In some cases students must pass an exam just to enter one of the big cram schools — which have spun off satellite *juku* to administer practice tests. Parental anxiety feeds the system, of course; as more students attend cram schools, more must go just to stay even.

At the stricter *juku* the instructors often act more like drill sergeants than teachers, instilling their little academic warriors with a spiritual fervor reminiscent of the mind-set that sent an earlier Japanese generation off to war. "Those without a fighting spirit, get out!" reads a slogan on the wall of one of these schools. *Juku* students often wear headbands like *kamikaze* pilots or samurai entering battle. If they make a mistake, they are browbeaten and humiliated before the class: "You're too soft! Get rid of your sloppy habits! Don't you have any fight in you?"

Parents who think that the younger generation is getting too soft applaud this return to old-fashioned discipline. Critics point out that the cram schools provide not an education but simply training in how to pass an exam. The critics also note that the *juku* undermine the principle that the examination system is based solely on merit: Students whose parents can afford the fees have a considerable advantage over children of families that cannot. Between 1961 and 1974 the percentage of students from the poorest two fifths of the population who got into the top universities dropped from 40 per cent to 27 per cent. At Tokyo University, the most prestigious institution of all, less than 1 per cent of entering students in recent years have come from blue-collar families.

"Struggle to pass," reads the band tied around the head of this boy, a pupil at a *juku*, or private cram school. There are more than 20,000 *juku* in Japan, attended by youngsters seeking a competitive edge in entrance exams for high schools and universities.

At best, the cram schools seem redundant. What they amount to, one expert on Japanese affairs has noted, is a remarkable instance of "a nation going to great lengths to supplement an already quite intense public education."

When the fateful February examination period finally arrives, tearful mothers exhort the students to do their best "so there will be no regrets." Families usually keep secret which exams their sons and daughters are taking; in the event of failure, public shame will be minimized. Most schools and universities post the results on bulletin boards — and nervous students go late at night to check the lists because they do not want to risk learning bad news in public. Every year some failed students take their own lives.

For the high school senior who is unable to get into the university of his choice, however, all is not quite lost: He can try again next year, and the next, for as long as his family's finances and his own fighting spirit hold out. One out of six high school graduates do fail and try again. A good proportion of them make it the second or third time around; they have lost a year or two, but once they are admitted to a university they are back on track.

Despite the criticism and the strain, it is clear that any student who has made it to a good high school or university has mastered a formidable body of knowledge. According to United Nations surveys, Japanese mathematics education is the best in the world, and international science tests have ranked Japanese youngsters fourth in the world in knowledge and first for ability to understand and apply what they know. Nor are the humanities neglected. Japanese high school students delve more deeply into the history, geogra-

LETTING OFF STEAM, JAPANESE STYLE

Dressed like Americans, teenagers dance their hearts out in the rain.

Sporting a haircut that is half punk, half samurai, a black-clad youth strums an imaginary guitar. The Japanese refer to such teenagers as *Amegurazoku*, after the film *American Graffiti*, the inspiration for their behavior.

To know how to conform is to know how to be Japanese. Young people are conditioned from earliest childhood to fit in; occasionally, however, some break loose, or at least they appear to. Among these are the boys and girls who flock to a part of central Tokyo dressed in fancy garb, much of it modeled on American teen-age fashions of the 1950s. There they cavort with one another, putting on dance numbers as if they were performers in a musical comedy.

But under their nonconformist behavior lies a rigid conformity. Every dance step is carefully rehearsed, each costume is meticulously assembled and gestures are worked out in advance. Some of the youths even engage in mock gang fights — without any of the combatants touching.

About all this there is something peculiarly Japanese. As one Japanese, a master of the tea ceremony with its prescribed ritual, put it, "Only when everybody acts the same do individual differences become apparent."

6

phy and culture of foreign countries than most other students around the world. All Japanese elementary school students learn how to read music, to play a simple musical instrument and to draw with a level of skill that in other countries would be considered evidence of innate artistic ability.

Japanese schools also strongly reinforce the pervasive belief that the group, and the nation, is more important than the individual. Classes in *dotoku,* moral education, impart the Confucian virtues of discipline, filial piety, loyalty and respect for the common good. The same virtues are taught in practice; the schoolchildren themselves are responsible for keeping their school clean (there are no janitors) and eagerly compete for the weekly prize awarded the neatest classroom.

Imbued with the group ethic, schoolchildren — especially boys — form tight little clubs devoted to some extracurricular activity, such as judo or model building. Members of these groups do everything together — studying, going to the movies or sitting around and talking. Friendships thus formed last for a lifetime. Regardless of their adult rank, these friends will always address one another with the familiar suffix *kun* instead of the usual honorific *san.*

The intensity of group feeling during the school years was demonstrated a few years ago when a teacher at one high school recommended an easier textbook to students who were having difficulty with the regular book. The students complained of discrimination; they wanted to keep the textbook that all other students of their level were using, even though they could not understand it. Reporting this incident, Kanji Nishio, a Japanese scholar, commented that "to force oneself to use a difficult

Attentive adults at a Tokyo school for culture learn *ikebana*, the art of flower arranging. Six million Japanese — mostly women — study *ikebana* each year; another 2.4 million take courses in the tea ceremony.

At a calligraphy contest, boys and girls apply themselves to limning free-flowing mottoes on scrolls. The winners are those who display fluid and bold brushwork.

textbook that one does not understand is hardly rational." Westerners, he said, would go their own way regardless of others, but his fellow Japanese, he declared, feel that "acting differently from others is unwise."

Getting into a Japanese university is the hard part; graduating is easy. Once a student enters a university, his future is settled; the pressure is off, and all he has to do now is play the game. No one has to worry about grades or graduating, since virtually no one flunks out. Only those studying technical subjects such as engineering have to work very hard or attend class regularly. True, the blue-chip firms will test applicants before hiring them, but students already adept at taking tests almost always pass the company examinations.

The content of university education has little bearing on future success. Japanese companies and government ministries hire on the basis of the university an applicant has attended, not on what was learned there. Far and away the most impressive diploma is one from Tokyo University. Only 3 per cent of all Japanese university students attend the institution, but its alumni make up one quarter of all the presidents of Japan's major corporations and almost the entire leadership of the Foreign Ministry.

Since it matters so little what grades their students get, the universities have tended to rest on their reputations, making little effort to improve teaching or to inspire those they teach. Rigid curricula and crowded classrooms discourage and bore the students, who, in the absence of challenge, become involved in outlandish fads, radical politics and even terrorism. It was student members of a radical group called the Red Army Faction, for example, who were responsible for the 1972 murder

MARRYING IN STYLE

Surrounded by family, a bride and groom have their wedding picture taken.

As elsewhere in the world, marriage in Japan is a ritual — and it can be a very expensive one. The families of both bride and groom share the cost of weddings. In one recent year they laid out $17 billion for knot-tying festivities, which works out to $22,000 a couple. Posters in Tokyo subways, featuring demure brides and dapper grooms, offer such cut-rate packages as the Shining Love ceremony ($2,500), performed in a small chapel at a deluxe hotel. At the other extreme are some truly astronomical figures: For example, the marriage of a champion sumo wrestler named Chionofuji cost $580,000. His bride's three kimonos alone cost $370,000.

of 26 people at Israel's Lod Airport.

Many Japanese blame the poor quality of the nation's universities on the U.S. Occupation's attempt to democratize higher education by giving hundreds of high schools and minor colleges university status. As the number of universities increased (fewer than a dozen in 1945, more than 500 today), standards naturally declined.

A more significant explanation of the mediocre performance of Japan's universities is lack of money. Eighty per cent of university students attend private universities, which receive little or no government support and few private gifts. (Japan has no tradition of charitable donations, and until recently the government gave no tax credit for them.) The private universities must get by on tuition fees alone, with the result that most of them are nearly bankrupt. Universities funded by public moneys are little better off; most

AN OLD AND HONORABLE WAY TO DIE

In a 19th Century reenactment of ritual suicide, the man in white, attended by friends, prepares to kill himself.

Suicide looms large in the Japanese psyche. This is because ritual suicide, or *seppuku* (cutting the belly), has been practiced in Japan for centuries (although it is no longer common). No shame is attached to the act. It is viewed, as one Japanese commentator has said, "as the ultimate justification," a way of saving face. During World War II, *seppuku* was committed by thousands of Imperial soldiers who refused to surrender or be captured; through this self-willed act, they preserved their honor and became — in Japanese eyes — victorious in defeat.

Seppuku is carried out in a prescribed manner. Holding his sword (or knife) along the blade, the individual takes a deep breath and inserts no more than three tenths of the blade into his belly in order to avoid piercing the intestine, which would cause excruciating pain. He yanks the blade to the right. He then positions the blade against the carotid artery in his neck and slashes it. If he has an assistant, as in the photograph above, the assistant administers the *coup de grâce* — a swift blow to the neck with a second sharp sword.

government educational subsidies go to enhancing the excellence of the public elementary and secondary schools.

Whatever the reasons, university education in Japan amounts to a four-year hiatus between high school and the rigors of a job — a welcome period of decompression. And the big Japanese companies do not mind. They regard it as their job to teach new employees what they need to know and to supply any postgraduate study that may be necessary. The big firms and the government bureaucracies enroll employees in many kinds of institutions and courses. Future production managers may take advanced courses in engineering; individuals who will work on the financial side of a corporation may study economics or banking; trading companies teach their employees foreign languages; and prospective corporate officers may be sent abroad to get master's degrees in business administration. They all collect company salaries while studying full time.

Obviously, few ambitious students would enroll in a foreign college or university on their own; that would not mesh with the Japanese hierarchical system and would destroy any chances for a significant career. But modern business and technology often require foreign training, so Japanese companies willingly send their young employees all over the globe for intensive study in the sciences, agriculture, business, social systems, languages and many other subjects — just as the Meiji government did in the 1880s.

Every year, for example, the Foreign Ministry dispatches two or three young officers to Peking to study Chinese language, culture and politics. Two years later one of those young officers will be sent to the U.S. and one to the Soviet

Union to immerse themselves in American and Soviet studies on China — and to pick up some general familiarity with the superpowers. Then, still considered apprentices, they may go back to Peking or to Hong Kong to help analyze current events. By this time the officers have become China experts, and only then will they be appointed to a responsible diplomatic post. Similar programs are carried out in other significant fields. Immediately after the 1973 oil crisis, hundreds of young Japanese from the government and the private sector showed up in the Middle East to learn Arabic and become familiar with Arab culture.

In the case of the Foreign Ministry, as everywhere else, such education is designed to further society's interests, not to satisfy the student's curiosity or inclinations. The willing acceptance of this

principle by modern Japanese testifies to the effectiveness of their training.

Whatever foreign views may be, the Japanese do not see themselves as bland products of social conditioning. They regard their inner discipline as a valuable asset that enables them to overcome any emotional, irrational or antisocial impulses that may arise within them. As one expert has put it, "Social conformity to the Japanese is no sign of weakness but rather the proud, tempered product of inner strength."

The Japanese are not in fact dull automatons, for all their devotion to their groups and their nation. The proof is in the miracle they have wrought in the 20th Century and especially since World War II, vastly elevating their country's position in the world and improving their own lives. For Japan, the system works. □

FINDING PEACE IN QUIET

Zen Buddhism is as much a part of Japanese life as rice. It pervades everything from art and architecture to sports, business and gardening. Yet while its influence is culturally dominant, its actual practice is limited to those with the perseverance to achieve inner peace and joy through active and regular meditation.

Among Zen Buddhism's most ardent adherents are the monks of the Soji Temple, near Yokohama. Members of the Soto order, one of three Zen sects in Japan, they practice a form of meditation called *zazen*. The monks sit with their legs folded beneath them, their backs straight and their hands in front of them, fingers and thumbs touching. They maintain this posture for as long as 45 minutes, two or three times a day.

During such sessions, two monitors walk up and down the rows of monks, each carrying a long, flat "awakening" stick. A monk about to doze off or one seeking to deepen his concentration may ask for a whack. "Pain," say the Buddhists, "is a form of thinking."

In line with the Buddhist belief that all people can achieve enlightenment, the monks regard even the most mundane activity as enabling them to realize their Buddhahood. Thus something as ordinary as eating or digging in the garden takes on spiritual meaning.

The monks earn most of their living by holding memorial and funeral services. They also operate a hospital and run several schools, including one for children whose parents want them to learn inner discipline.

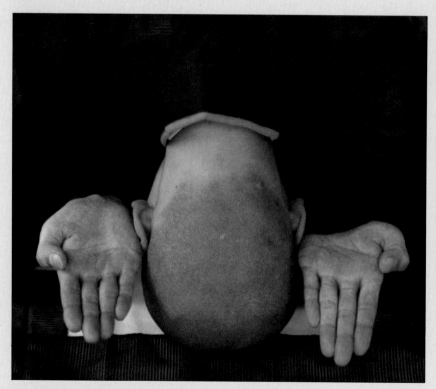

With upturned palms symbolizing open lotus petals, a Zen monk lowers his forehead to the floor in reverence. Such acts show gratitude to Buddha for sharing the spiritual path to truth.

148

**Monks at the Soji Temple face the wall
of the *zendo*, a long hall with tatami-
covered platforms on each side, where
they practice sitting meditation.**

In the main ceremonial hall of the Soji Temple, four new priests in red robes perform their first memorial service. To become a priest, a monk must

devote five years to study and meditation.

Manual labor such as weeding the temple garden is part of a novice's daily meditative activity.

A novice glides down a hallway, polishing the wooden floor with rags held beneath his hands. The chore is performed three times a day.

Wielding brooms, novices clean the grounds in front of the double-roofed hall where large effigies of Buddha and two of his disciples are enshrined.

A Zen master delivers a slap of the awakening stick to the shoulders of a girl, correcting her posture during a half hour of *zazen*. The children attend

the temple-run class once a week to receive training in meditation.

ACKNOWLEDGMENTS

The index was prepared by Barbara L. Klein. For their help with this book, the editors thank: Fernando Afable, Washington, D.C.; Kazuhiro and Naoko Akimoto, Astronomy Program, University of Maryland, College Park, Md.; Nobuo Hatakenaka, Labor Attaché, Embassy of Japan, Washington, D.C.; Shojo Honda, Senior Reference Librarian, Japanese Section, Asian Division, Library of Congress, Washington, D.C.; Melanie Humphrey, Japan Economic Institute of America, Washington, D.C.; Ine Fisheries Cooperative, Kyoto Prefecture, Japan; Roshi Jiyu-Kennett, Shasta Abbey, Mount Shasta, Calif.; Arthur E. Klauser, Senior Vice President, Mitsui & Co. (U.S.A.), Ltd., Washington, D.C.; Maki and Associates, Tokyo; David R. McAuliffe, President and Representative Director, Time-Life Books Japan Inc., Tokyo; Nerima Agricultural Cooperative Association, Tokyo; Gene Norrett, Dataquest, San Jose, Calif.; Yasuyori Okuda, Alexandria, Va.; Ford Park, Xerox Corporation, Stamford, Conn.; Ken Shimba, Public Relations, Matsushita Electrical Industrial Co., Ltd., Secaucus, N.J.; Larry Suter, National Center for Education Statistics, U.S. Dept. of Education, Washington, D.C.; Seiichi Toshida, Economic Counselor, Embassy of Japan, Washington, D.C.; Norihisa Yamamoto, Editor, *President Magazine*, Tokyo. These sources were particularly valuable: *The Japanese* by Edwin O. Reischauer, The Belknap Press of Harvard University, © 1977; *The Japanese Mind: The Goliath Explained* by Robert C. Christopher, Linden Press/Simon and Schuster, © 1983; "Life on the Fast Line" by John Junkerman, in *Mother Jones*, August 1982; "Japan Inc. Goes International" in *Business Week*, Dec. 14, 1983. Quoted material is reprinted from *Long Engagements: Maturity in Modern Japan* by David W. Plath with permission of the publishers, Stanford University Press, © 1980 by the Board of Trustees of the Leland Stanford Junior University.

PICTURE CREDITS

Credits from left to right are separated by semicolons, from top to bottom by dashes.

Cover: Paul Chesley. Front and back endpaper maps: Lloyd K. Townsend. Back endpaper map: Digitized by Graphic and Design Computer Services.

1, 2: © Flag Research Center, Winchester, Massachusetts. 6, 7: © Kaku Kurita/Gamma-Liaison; inset map by Sam Haltom of Another Color, Inc. Digitized by Graphic and Design Services, London. 8, 9: © Dennis Stock/Magnum; inset chart by Sam Haltom of Another Color, Inc. Digitized by Graphic and Design Services, London. 10, 11: © Richard Kalvar/Magnum. 12, 13: Ethan Hoffman; inset chart by Sam Haltom of Another Color, Inc. Digitized by Graphic and Design Services, London. 14, 15: © Kaku Kurita/Gamma-Liaison; inset chart by Sam Haltom of Another Color, Inc. Digitized by Graphic and Design Services, London. 16, 17: © 1983 Gary Braasch. 18, 19: Thomas Höpker/Agentur Anne Hamann, Munich. 21: Sankei Shimbun, Tokyo. 22: Manabu Watabe, Tokyo. 24, 25: Thomas Höpker/Woodfin Camp; © Harald Sund. 26: © Kaku Kurita/Gamma-Liaison. 27: © Harald Sund. 28, 29: Yasunobu Takagi, Tokyo — T. Tanuma/Sports Illustrated; Robert Lebeck/STERN, Hamburg. 31: Drawings by Sam Haltom of Another Color, Inc. 32: Denis Waugh, London.

33-43: Ethan Hoffman. 44: Atsuo Akanuma, Nagano Prefecture, Japan. 46, 47: Paul Chesley/Aspen. 48, 49: Paul Chesley/Aspen; Kate Bader. 50, 51: Paul Chesley/Aspen. 52: Carl Mydans for *Life*. 53: Shosaburo Hiraoka, Kagoshima, Japan. 54: Paul Chesley/Aspen. 55: Fred Maroon. 56, 57: Yasuhiro Ishimoto, Tokyo. 58: Paul Chesley/Aspen. 59: © Brian Brake from Photo Researchers. 60, 61: Henebry Photography; Yasuhiro Ishimoto, Tokyo. 62, 63: Eberhard Grames/Bilderberg, Hamburg. 64-73: Ethan Hoffman. 74, 75: Burton Holmes Collection. 76: Bradley Smith. 77: Imperial Household Agency, Tokyo. 78: Ishiyama Temple, Otsu, Japan; Bradley Smith (2); The Okura Shukokan Museum, Tokyo. 79: Library of Congress — Kanagawa Prefectural Museum, Yokohama; Kyodo News Service, Tokyo. 81: Imperial Household Agency, Tokyo. 82: Kobe Municipal Museum, Kobe, Japan. 83: L. J. Anderson Collection/Werner Forman Archive, London — from *The Sword and the Samé* by Henri L. Joly and Inada Hogitaro, Charles E. Tuttle, New York, 1963. 84: Woodblock by Hiroshige from the collection of Robert Vergez, photographed by Kaku Kurita, Tokyo. 85: The Meiji Memorial Picture Gallery, Tokyo. 86: Private collection. 87: UPI. 88, 89: U.S. Navy Photo. 90, 91: Minoru Akiyama, Tokyo. 92: Eberhard Grames/Bilderberg, Hamburg. 93: Idemitsu Art Gallery, Tokyo. 94: Hideyuki Oka, Tokyo (2) — Takeji Iwamiya, Osaka. 95: Drawings by Sam Haltom of Another Color, Inc. 96, 97: © Harald Sund. 98, 99: Reinhart Wolf, Hamburg. 101: Kaneaki Monma, Tokyo. 102: Courtesy of the Freer Gallery of Art, Smithsonian Institution, Washington, D.C. 103: The Bridgeman Art Library, courtesy the Trustees of the British Museum, London. 104-105: Ethan Hoffman. 106: James Moore. 107: Fujio Fujiko, Tokyo. 108, 109: Tom Jacobi/STERN, Hamburg. 110-111: Tom Jacobi/STERN, Hamburg (2); Kenneth Love. 112, 113: Tom Jacobi/STERN, Hamburg. 114, 115: Tom Jacobi/STERN, Hamburg; Kazuhiko Ohori, Tokyo (2). 116, 117: Yoshitaka Nakatani, Tokyo. 119: Masachika Suhara for *Fortune*. 120: Ethan Hoffman. 121: Xerox Corporation. 123: Asahi Shimbun, Tokyo, courtesy Professor Shoji Tatsukawa, Kawasaki, Japan. 124: Andreas Dannenberg/Woodfin Camp. 125: Mark Wexler/Jullien Photo Agency; Andreas Dannenberg/Woodfin Camp — Keiichi Hirayama, Tokyo. 126: © Nik Wheeler. 127: Drawing by K. F. Scherr Illustration. 129: Ethan Hoffman/Archive Pictures. 130: Japan Press Photo, Tokyo. 132, 133: Thomas Höpker/Woodfin Camp. 135: Ethan Hoffman. 137: Thomas Höpker/Agentur Anne Hamann, Munich. 138, 139: Roger Archibald/Woodfin Camp; Toshitaka Morita from Bon Color, Tokyo — Paul Chesley/Aspen. 140, 141: Thomas Höpker/Woodfin Camp (2) — Ethan Hoffman; Yoshio Watanabe, Tokyo; Ethan Hoffman. 142: Masachika Suhara/*Discover*. 143: Ethan Hoffman. 144: Tom Jacobi/STERN, Hamburg — Claude Charlier/A.N.A., Paris. 145: Thomas Höpker/Woodfin Camp. 146: Übersee Museum, Bremen, photo STERN Books, Hamburg. 147: Fred Seidman. 148-155: Ethan Hoffman.

BIBLIOGRAPHY

BOOKS

Aoki, Michiko Y., and Margaret B. Dardess, *As the Japanese See It.* Honolulu: The University Press of Hawaii, 1981.

Bauer, Helen, and Sherwin Carlquist, *Japanese Festivals.* Garden City, N.Y.: Doubleday, 1965.

Beasley, William G., *The Meiji Restoration.* Stanford, Calif.: Stanford University Press, 1972.

Benedict, Ruth, *The Chrysanthemum and the Sword: Patterns of Japanese Culture.* Boston: Houghton Mifflin, 1946.

Blyth, R. H., *A History of Haiku*, Vol. 1. New York: The Hokuseido Press, 1963.

Bunge, Frederica M., ed., *Japan: A Country Study* (Area Handbook series). Washington, D.C.: United States Government, 1982.

Burks, Arduth W., *Profile of a Postindustrial Power.* Boulder, Colo.: Westview Press, 1981.

Christopher, Robert C., *The Japanese Mind: The Goliath Explained.* New York: Linden Press/Simon and Schuster, 1983.

Cody, Billy J., "Unifiers of Japan," in *Great Historical Figures of Japan*, Murakami Hyoe and Thomas J. Harper, eds. Tokyo: Japan Culture Institute, 1978.

Cole, Robert E., *Japanese Blue Collar, The Changing Tradition.* Berkeley, Calif.: University of California Press, 1971.

Cummings, William, Ikuo Amano and Kazuyuki Kitamura, *Changes in the Japanese University.* New York: Praeger, 1979.

Curtis, Gerald, *Election Campaigning Japanese Style.* New York: Columbia University Press, 1971.

Decker, Robert and Barbara, *Volcanoes.* San Francisco: W. H. Freeman, 1981.

DeMente, Boye, *The Japanese Way of Doing Business.* Englewood Cliffs, N.J.: Prentice-Hall, 1981.

Dore, Ronald P., *Shinohata: A Portrait of a Japanese Village.* New York: Pantheon, 1978.

Facts and Figures of Japan. 1982 edition. Tokyo: Kinji Kawamura, Foreign Press Center, 1982.

Fairbank, John K., and Edwin O. Reischauer:
East Asia: The Great Tradition. Boston: Houghton Mifflin, 1960.
East Asia: The Modern Transformation. Boston: Houghton Mifflin, 1965.

The Far East and Australasia, 1982-1983. London: Europa Publications Limited, 1982.

Forbis, William H., *Japan Today: People, Places, Power.* New York: Harper & Row, 1975.

Fukutake, Tadashi, *Japanese Society Today.* Tokyo: University of Tokyo Press, 1974.

Hall, John Whitney, and Richard K. Beardsley, *Twelve Doors to Japan.* New York: McGraw-Hill, 1965.

Halloran, Richard, *Japan: Images and Realities.* New York: Random House, 1969.

Hane, Mikiso, *Peasants, Rebels and Outcasts: The Underside of Modern Japan.* New York: Pantheon, 1982.

Henderson, Harold G., *An Introduction to Haiku.* New York: Doubleday, 1958.

Hibbett, Howard, *The Floating World in Japanese Fiction.* London: Oxford University Press, 1959.

Hillier, Jack, *Utamaro: Colour Prints and Paintings.* Oxford: Phaidon, 1961.

Huddle, Norie, and Michael Reich, *Island of Dreams.* Tokyo: Autumn Press, 1975.

Inoura, Yoshinobu, and Toshio Kawatake, *The Traditional Theatre of Japan.* New York and Tokyo: Weatherhill, 1971.

International Bank for Reconstruction and Development/World Bank, *World Development Report 1983*. New York: Oxford University Press for the World Bank, 1983.

Ito, Hirobumi, "Some Reminiscences on the Grant of the New Constitution," in *Fifty Years of New Japan* (compiled by Shigenobu Okuma; English version edited by Marcus B. Huish), Vol. 1. London: Smith, Elder, 1910.

Japan Foundation, *Japanstyle*. San Francisco: Kodansha International, 1980.

Japan Institute for Social and Economic Affairs, *Japan 1982, An International Comparison*. Tokyo: Keizai Koho Center, 1982.

Jensen, Marius B., "Introduction to the History of Japan," in *Japan: A History in Art*, Bradley Smith, ed. Japan: Gemini, 1964.

Johnson, Chalmers, *MITI and the Japanese Miracle: The Growth of Industrial Policy, 1925-1975*. Stanford, Calif.: Stanford University Press, 1982.

Kamata, Satoshi, *Japan in the Passing Lane*. New York: Pantheon, 1982.

Kawabata, Yasunari, *Snow Country*. Transl. by Edward G. Seidensticker. New York: Berkley Publishing Corporation, 1968.

Kawai, Kazuo, *Japan's American Interlude*. Chicago: The University of Chicago Press, 1960.

Keene, Donald:
Japanese Literature. New York: Grove Press, 1955.
Landscapes and Portraits: Appreciations of Japanese Culture. Palo Alto, Calif.: Kodansha International, 1971.

Lebra, Joyce, Joy Paulson and Elizabeth Powers, eds., *Women in Changing Japan*. Stanford, Calif.: Stanford University Press, 1976.

Leonard, Jonathan N., *Early Japan*. New York: Time-Life Books, 1968.

Macintyre, Michael, *The Shogun Inheritance*. London: William Collins Sons & Co. Ltd. and the British Broadcasting Corporation, 1981.

Masatsugu, Mitsuyuki, *The Modern Samurai Society*. New York: American Management Associations, 1982.

Mast, Gerald, *A Short History of the Movies*. Indianapolis: Bobbs-Merrill, 1976.

Mellen, Joan:
Voices from the Japanese Cinema. New York: Liveright, 1975.
The Waves at Genji's Door — Japan through Its Cinema. New York: Pantheon, 1976.

Nakane, Chie, *Japanese Society*. Berkeley and Los Angeles: University of California Press, 1970.

Narazaki, Muneshige, *Hokusai: "The Thirty-Six Views of Mt. Fuji."* Tokyo: Kodansha, 1968.

Peters, Thomas J., and Robert H. Waterman Jr., *In Search of Excellence: Lessons from America's Best-Run Corporations*. New York: Harper & Row, 1982.

Plath, David W., *Long Engagements — Maturity in Modern Japan*. Stanford, Calif.: Stanford University Press, 1980.

Reischauer, Edwin O.:
Japan: Past and Present. New York: Knopf, 1964.
Japan: The Story of a Nation. New York: Knopf, 1974.
The Japanese. Cambridge, Mass.: Belknap Press of Harvard University, 1977.

Richie, Donald:
The Films of Akira Kurosawa. Berkeley, Calif.: University of California Press, 1973.
The Inland Sea. New York: Weatherhill, 1971.

Roberts, John G., *Mitsui: Three Centuries of Japanese Business*. New York/Tokyo: Weatherhill, 1973.

Rohlen, Thomas P.:
For Harmony and Strength. Berkeley, Calif.: University of California Press, 1974.
Japan's High Schools. Berkeley, Calif.: University of

California Press, 1983.

Sakiya, Tetsuo, *Honda Motor: The Men, the Management, the Machines*. Transl. by Kiyoshi Ikemi. New York: Kodansha, 1982.

Scalapino, Robert A., and Junnosuke Masumi, *Parties and Politics in Contemporary Japan*. Berkeley and Los Angeles: University of California Press, 1967.

Scott, A. C., *The Theatre in Asia*. New York: Macmillan, 1972.

Smith, Robert J., *Kurusu: The Price of Progress in a Japanese Village, 1951-1975*. Stanford, Calif.: Stanford University Press, 1978.

Statistics Bureau, Prime Minister's Office, *Statistical Handbook of Japan, 1982*. Tokyo: Japan Statistical Association, 1982.

Terry, Thomas Philip, *Terry's Guide to the Japanese Empire*. Boston and New York: Houghton Mifflin, 1933.

The Editors of Time-Life Books, *The Aftermath: Asia* (World War II series). Alexandria, Va.: Time-Life Books, 1983.

Toita, Yasuji, *Kabuki — The Popular Theater*. New York, Tokyo: Weatherhill/Tokansha, 1970.

Trewartha, Glenn T., *Japan: A Geography*. Madison, Wis.: The University of Wisconsin Press, 1965.

Totman, Conrad D., *Japan Before Perry: A Short History*. Berkeley, Calif.: University of California Press, 1981.

Vogel, Ezra F.:
Japan as Number One: Lessons for America. New York: Harper & Row, 1979.
Japan's New Middle Class — The Salary Man and His Family in a Tokyo Suburb. Berkeley, Calif.: University of California Press, 1965.

Waley, Arthur, *The No Plays of Japan*. New York: Grove Press, 1957.

Watanabe, Yasutada, *Shinto Art: Ise and Izumo Shrines*. Transl. by Robert Ricketts. New York, Tokyo: Weatherhill/Heibonsha, 1974.

Whitford, Frank, *Japanese Prints and Western Painters*. New York: Macmillan, 1977.

Yanaga, Chitoshi, *Japan Since Perry*. Westport, Conn.: Greenwood Press, 1975.

Yoshioka, Yutaka, *Food and Agriculture in Japan*. Tokyo: Kinji Kawamura, Foreign Press Center, 1979.

PERIODICALS AND OTHER SOURCES

Berger, Michael, "Japanese Women — Old Images and New Realities." *Japan Interpreter*, Spring 1976.

Bock, Audie, "American Directors Look East to Japan for Inspiration and Art." *The New York Times*, October 5, 1980.

Buell, Barbara, "Corporate Boot Camp in Japan." *Life*, September 1983.

Bylinsky, Gene, "The Race to Automate the Factory." *Fortune*, February 21, 1983.

Christopher, Robert D., "Japan's Media-mad Society." *Asia*, July/August 1983.

"Dix Dates pour une Histoire du Cinéma Japonais." *Zoom*, Spécial Japon, Paris, 1982.

Graves, William, "Living in a Japanese Village." *National Geographic*, May 1972.

Halberstam, David, "Bonsai: The Tree That Explains the Japanese Spirit." *Geo*, October 1983.

Hough, Richard, "The Difficult Journey: I — Off to the Holy War; II — Magnificent but Foul; III — Battle." *The New Yorker*, October 11, 18 and 25, 1958.

"How Japan Does It," *Time*, March 30, 1981.

Jack, Michael, "Japanese Film Greats at AFI." *Washington Star*, November 3, 1974.

"Japan: A Nation in Search of Itself." Special issue of *Time*, August 1, 1983.

"Japan Inc. Goes International." *Business Week*, December 14, 1981.

Junkerman, John, "Life on the Fast Line at Datsun." *Mother Jones*, August 1982.

Kamata, Satoshi, "The Tyranny of the Line: A Toyota Worker's Story." *Asia*, November/December 1982.

Kuwayama, Patricia Hagan, "Success Story." *The Wilson Quarterly*, Winter 1982.

Lee, Douglas, "Japan's Last Frontier: Hokkaido." *National Geographic*, January 1980.

Matsubara, Hisako, "This Good World of Shinto." *Geo*, March 1981.

Mellen, Joan, "The Cinematic Search for the Japanese Spirit." *The New York Times*, April 10, 1977.

Mills, David O., "The Idioms of Contemporary Japan XVI — Kiseru-josha." *Japan Interpreter*, Autumn 1976.

Nishio, Kanji, "Avoiding Competition: Its Merits and Contradictions." *Japan Echo*, 1979.

"Popular Culture." Special issue of *Japan Echo*, 1980.

Rohlen, Thomas P., "The *Juku* Phenomenon: An Exploratory Essay." *The Journal of Japanese Studies*, Summer 1980.

Scott Stokes, Henry, "Japan's Love Affair with the Robot." *The New York Times Magazine*, January 10, 1982.

Skinner, Kenneth A., "Salaryman Comics in Japan: Images of Self-Perception." *Journal of Popular Culture*, Summer 1979.

Vogel, Suzanne H., "Professional Housewife: The Career of Urban Middle Class Japanese Women." *The Japan Interpreter*, Winter 1978.

"A Wedding Every 20 Minutes," *Time*, December 6, 1982.

"Women in Japan's Workforce." *JEI Report*, Japan Economic Institute, July 29, 1983.

INDEX

Page numbers in italics refer to illustrations or illustrated text.

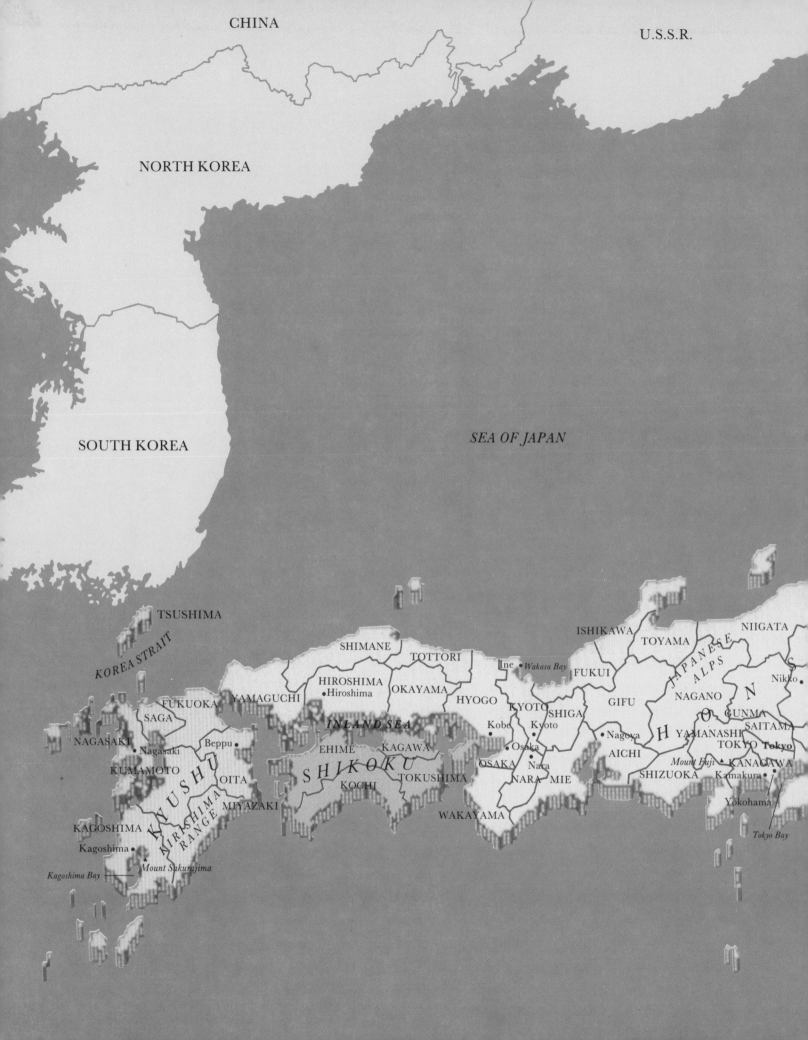